THE LITTLE BOOK OF

Racial Healing

Published titles include:

THE LITTLE BOOK OF

Racial Healing

*Coming to the Table for Truth-Telling,
Liberation, and Transformation*

THOMAS NORMAN DEWOLF AND JODIE GEDDES

Good Books

New York, New York

Table of Contents

1.
Introduction

On a brisk, sunny Seattle day in February 2017, family and friends gathered to celebrate the life of Susan Hutchison, who had passed from this life two months prior. People who walked with Susan along the various paths she had traveled throughout her life's journey shared stories of their times together. The common thread was Susan's commitment to truth, healing, and love. Squi qui Ray Williams, a Swinomish elder of the Coastal Salish People who shared in prayer, drumming, and song, said that in remembering Susan, we were *"re-membering"* her; putting her back together through our memories and stories.

A direct descendant of President Thomas Jefferson, Susan knew her family's long, deep connection to slavery. In 2003, she attended a gathering of descendants of Jefferson and his wife, Martha, and those of Jefferson and the woman he enslaved, Sally Hemings. The attendees built friendships and embraced each other as family and cousins, affectionately referring to themselves as "Sallys" and "Marthas." In her quest to meet more descendants of families who had enslaved people, she met Will Hairston, a descendant of one of the largest enslaving empires in the Old South. Susan and Will dreamed of a "family reunion" in which descendants of people who were enslavers gathered with descendants of people their ancestors had enslaved. They believed that as people built relationships with those on the "other side," the deep, historic wounds engendered by the legacy of slavery could be confronted and potentially healed.

Dr. Kofi Anyidoho, of the University of Ghana, describes the present-day consequences of slavery as "a tragic accident in which people today are still bleeding to death. Slavery is a living wound, under a patchwork of scars."[1] After 245 years of slavery in the United States and 100 years of government-sanctioned, discriminatory Jim Crow laws, the "living wound" is evident among people of color, who fall on the negative side of virtually all measurable social indicators relative to white people. Professor Anyidoho concluded, "The only hope of healing is to be willing to break through the scars to finally clean the wound properly and begin the healing."[2]

Susan and Will were inspired to begin this healing by Dr. Martin Luther King Jr.'s words, spoken from the steps of the Lincoln Memorial in Washington, DC, on August 28, 1963: "I have a dream that one day on the red hills of Georgia the sons of former slaves and the sons of former slave owners will be able to sit down together at the table of brotherhood." They invited black and white cousins, Jeffersons and Hairstons, to join them in planning a radical new approach to support and guide people in our struggle with racism.

In 2006, Coming to the Table (CTTT) was born when two dozen of these cousins gathered together at

Eastern Mennonite University (EMU). They shared stories and developed deep and important friendships. Participants conceived a vision of a more connected, just, and truthful society that would acknowledge and seek to heal the unresolved and persistent racial wounds of the past that continue to affect and harm all of us today. The damage to people and communities of color are obvious. It is also important to recognize the wounds of separation, division, guilt, and shame that white people carry. Since that first gathering, CTTT has grown into a community of thousands across the United States and around the world. In these challenging times, efforts like CTTT are needed now more than ever.

The Approach

This Little Book introduces Coming to the Table's approach to moving toward this vision. The approach represents a continuously evolving set of purposeful theories, ideas, experiments, guidelines, and intentions, all dedicated to facilitating racial healing and transformation. You might think of this approach as a recipe that has been evolving within a growing family for generations. A recipe with ingredients that change over time as new ideas sprout up as more people participate. A recipe for a meal we create together and bring to the table to nourish and support our beloved family.

The CTTT approach initially grew out of the STAR program (Strategies for Trauma Awareness and Resilience) at the Center for Justice & Peacebuilding (CJP) at EMU. The work of CTTT stands on this foundation of trauma awareness as well as that of restorative justice and follows a process supported by four interrelated pillars:

- **Pillar 1:** Uncover History—Research, acknowledge, and share personal, family, community, and national histories of race.
- **Pillar 2:** Make Connections—Connect with others within and across racial lines and build authentic and accountable relationships.
- **Pillar 3:** Work Toward Healing—Explore how we can heal together, using a variety of methods.
- **Pillar 4:** Take Action—Actively champion systemic and structural change throughout our society and in all aspects of life to support equality, justice, and healing for all.

The following pages introduce you to the foundations of racial healing in trauma awareness and restorative justice, with a chapter devoted to each of the pillars described above. A chapter on circle processes offers tools for effective communication when making connections (Pillar 2).

Why are we the two to write this book? The genesis came after we co-facilitated a breakout session at a 2016 restorative justice conference. In conversation with other restorative justice practitioners, we agreed to contribute some writing to the field to help support the understanding that "race" is critically important in any and all conversations about justice in the United States. We also represent two "sides" of the history and conversation about race.

As a Jamaican native having grown up in Brooklyn, Jodie uses her story as a catalyst for transforming systems. As of this writing, she serves as the community organizing coordinator at Restorative Justice for Oakland Youth (RJOY) and leads RJOY's national

Truth-telling, Racial Healing, and Reparations Project. Additionally, she is a trainer and facilitator of restorative processes in schools, justice systems, and communities. Jodie speaks nationally on the subject of restorative justice, truth processes, and reparation, and is a published poet and writer, with her work featured on the online platforms *For Harriet* and *Blavity.* She earned an MA in conflict transformation from CJP and serves as president of the board of managers for Coming to the Table.

Tom is related to the largest slave-trading dynasty in US history. His first book, *Inheriting the Trade,* is the story of his experiences in the making of the Emmy-nominated PBS documentary *Traces of the Trade: A Story from the Deep North,* in which he and nine distant cousins retraced the triangle slave trade route of their ancestors and grappled with the present-day consequences of the legacy of slavery. He is a co-author, with Sharon Morgan, of *Gather at the Table: The Healing Journey of a Daughter of Slavery and a Son of the Slave Trade.* Tom serves as executive director for Coming to the Table and is a trained STAR practitioner.

We recognize "racial healing" is a *big* topic for a little book. We do not intend this book to be an exhaustive representation of racial healing theories or options, or an "all-or-nothing" approach. We trust the ideas and resources presented here will complement and/or apply to other social and racial justice approaches. You may find some elements more useful than others and develop alternatives that better fit your context. At the end of the book, we have included a wide variety of recommended additional reading for further study.

Overall, we hope this Little Book inspires struggle, curiosity, and wonder as well as a desire to grapple with concepts of racial transformation, liberation, and healing. We consider these pages a starting place from which to transform individual hearts and minds, the communities in which we all live, and unjust systems and structures. With our collective intentions and good work, we can transform our world.

Re-membering

Ray Williams, the Swinomish elder who guided our re-membering of our deceased friend, Susan, said she was with us in the church that day, along with other ancestors. You could feel and see them, standing tall above Ray as he spoke. "Mom Shay" was surely there. Shay Banks-Young and Susan were cousins; a "Sally" and a "Martha" who loved and supported each other and helped plan and lead the first CTTT gathering. Shay, who passed away six months before Susan, was a tireless civil rights activist, spoke nationally on racial harmony and genealogy, and never wavered in her commitment and service to CTTT and her "linked descendants" from slavery days. Susan and Shay leave us with a powerful legacy—and responsibility. Ray encouraged everyone at Susan's service to conduct our lives so that the ancestors know we are paying attention:

> They are in a place of pure knowing. They want to share what they know with us. When we have ears to hear, eyes to see, and when our hearts are open, they have gifts for us; gifts that will help us. There is a lot more to life than we often are aware.

The ancestors, including Susan and Shay, ask us to truly believe in our gifts, whatever they may be: loving, singing, writing, organizing. They invite us to be open to receive our gifts from the ancestors and to carry on the work of healing. We have the opportunity to show up, show what we have learned, and show what we can do.

Let it be so.

2.
Trauma Awareness and Resilience

"As human beings we belong to an extremely resilient species. Since time immemorial we have rebounded from our relentless wars, countless disasters (both natural and man-made), and the violence and betrayal in our own lives. But traumatic experiences do leave traces, whether on a large scale (on our histories and cultures) or close to home, on our families, with dark secrets being imperceptibly passed down through generations. They also leave traces on our minds and emotions, on our capacity for joy and intimacy, and even on our biology and immune systems. Trauma affects not only those who are directly exposed to it, but also on those around them."[1]

— Bessel van der Kolk, M.D.

We began to write this chapter two days after seventeen people were shot and killed by a young man firing an AR-15 semiautomatic rifle at Marjory Stoneman Douglas High School in Parkland, Florida.

School shootings. Police shootings of unarmed black people. Terrorist attacks. Domestic violence. Deadly hurricanes and earthquakes. War. Famine. Fatal accidents. Genocide. Disease. Homelessness.

Trauma.

The word *trauma* means *wound*. It is different from stress, which is normal, can feel positive or negative, and, at certain levels, can lead to creativity and productivity. Too much stress results in distress, which can lead to frustration, anxiety, and disease. Traumatic stress is an emotional wound that results from experiencing a highly stressful, horrifying event over which one feels they have no control; in which one feels powerless and threatened by injury or death to oneself or others. Trauma is "when our ability to respond to a threat is overwhelmed."[2] Trauma hits us where we are most vulnerable. Whatever order exists in our lives becomes chaos.

We may experience trauma as individuals in response to things that happen to us or situations or events in which we participate. Trauma may result from secondary or vicarious experiences, as well as dignity violations. We may experience trauma collectively, through historical, generational, and cultural events, as well as from ongoing, structural/systemic forces. Trauma can result from a single event or from continuous and cumulative events.

Becoming trauma-informed is key to racial healing. We offer here the briefest of introductions, focusing on the impact of trauma on our bodies, brains, and nervous and energy systems. We draw on the STAR (Strategies for Trauma Awareness and Resilience) approach to trauma healing, which connects individual and collective healing with organizational and societal

9

well-being. Carolyn Yoder, founding director of STAR, points out that ". . . traumatic events and times have the potential to awaken the best of the human spirit and, indeed, the global family . . . At the core, [trauma healing] is spiritual work of the deepest sort, calling forth nothing less than the noblest ideals and the faith, hope, and resilience of the human spirit."[3]

To reach that potential, we must acknowledge our own history, the history of "the other," search honestly for root causes of trauma, and place our emphasis on the healing, liberation, and transformation of all of us.

Traumatic Response

STAR teaches that trauma is an inevitable part of life. Our brains are designed to orchestrate responses to trauma that aim to protect us and keep us safe. The amygdala, located in the *emotional* brain (limbic system), sends a message to the *instinctual* (or "lizard") brain (brain stem), which then responds with fight, flight, or freeze. This is automatic/instinctual and happens before the rational/thinking portion of our brain (cerebral cortex) can engage. Rational thought is basically bypassed in times of traumatic stress to help us survive, which then affects brain function and group behavior. If we don't subsequently engage in rational thought, we cannot effectively address or heal from the trauma.

Unresolved Trauma

Unhealed trauma results in cycles of victimhood or violence that are fueled by reenactment. Current and future generations are harmed by these acting-in and acting-out behaviors (see Figure 1).

Figure 1.

Cycles of Violence

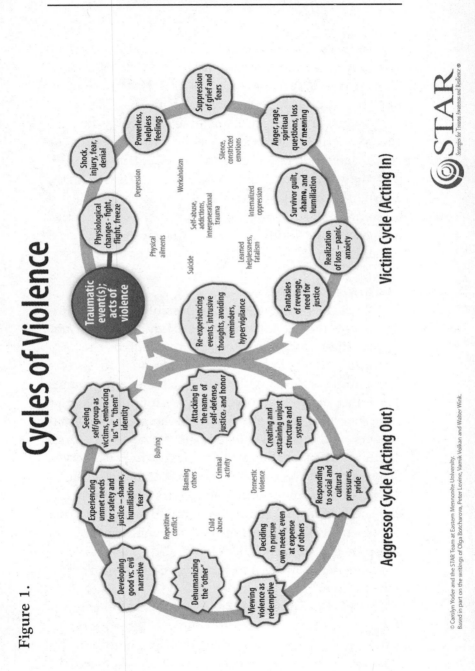

Victim Cycle (Acting In)

Aggressor Cycle (Acting Out)

© Carolyn Yoder and the STAR Team at Eastern Mennonite University.
Based in part on the writings of Olga Botcharova, Peter Levine, Vamik Volkan and Walter Wink.

Cycles of violence occur when an individual or group responds to violence with more violence; that is, hurt people hurt people. It is important to remember three points. First, a cycle of violence does not necessarily happen in a linear way, as may be perceived in the illustration. Second, an individual or group may not experience all of what is pictured, and they may experience several at the same time. Third, we may find ourselves (or our community or nation) at times on both cycles: those of victim *and* aggressor (both of which are destructive and unhealthy).

Trauma Healing

STAR teaches that healing is possible for individuals, communities, and societies. Human beings can engage their rational brains, be resilient in the face of trauma, and find ways to transcend and thrive. The same is true of communities. This healing comes from the bio-psycho way of viewing trauma and resilience and integrating it with the social-spiritual aspects of trauma (which will be discussed in more detail in future chapters). This integration also serves to prevent future trauma. An indicator of the healing process in the months and years after traumatic experiences is the quality of relationships—how we treat ourselves and our families, the concern for each other in our communities, and the peacefulness of our societies. Caring and peaceful communities prevent trauma.

Though the strategies listed below are too important to racial healing work to simply be listed without a thorough narrative context, we offer them here by way of introduction. These and other themes will show up in more detail in subsequent chapters within the context of restorative justice, circle process, and the four pillars.

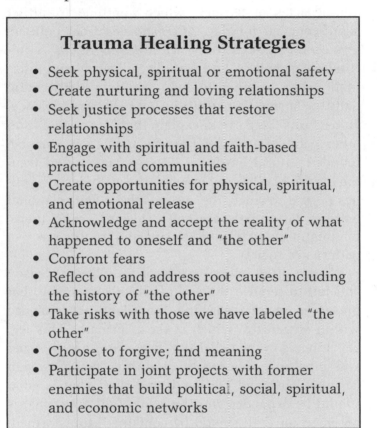

Trauma Healing Strategies

- Seek physical, spiritual or emotional safety
- Create nurturing and loving relationships
- Seek justice processes that restore relationships
- Engage with spiritual and faith-based practices and communities
- Create opportunities for physical, spiritual, and emotional release
- Acknowledge and accept the reality of what happened to oneself and "the other"
- Confront fears
- Reflect on and address root causes including the history of "the other"
- Take risks with those we have labeled "the other"
- Choose to forgive; find meaning
- Participate in joint projects with former enemies that build political, social, spiritual, and economic networks

Self-care is also a critical aspect of trauma healing, including racial trauma, as leaders and caregivers may be traumatized by the events themselves and/or by helping others. Self-care also attends to both the individual and the collective. In taking care of the self, the community is also served, as the individual builds a community of care that bridges "me care" and "we care."

Historic Trauma of Slavery

Racial healing requires a focus on the specific, historic trauma and unhealed wounds of the aftermath and legacies of slavery, which continue to inflict significant harm today. *Aftermath* describes political and economic structures, while *legacy* refers to cultural ideas, beliefs, and prejudices. Legacy and aftermath work together to help maintain detrimental cultural norms that result in, and sustain, violence. Hooker and Czajkowski explain that ". . . systems and other political and social arrangements are, thereby, founded in and based on trauma-causing and trauma-effected beliefs. Even when the attitudes and values (legacy) change, the systems, laws and relational patterns (aftermath) are much slower to shift, therefore maintaining trauma-causing and trauma-reactive patterns in society."[4]

We are often operating out of the place of legacy and fail to remove the veil of white supremacy that preserves racist ideas and the silence of violence within structures, which is the aftermath. This legacy adheres to the belief that Europeans are civilized and good and, as a result, everything non-European is uncivilized and not good, and that what is good should be expanded "for the good of all" and what is not good (or evil) should be contained, transformed, or extinguished.[5] The resulting aftermath consisted of laws enabling enslavement in Europe and the Americas.

The history of the United States is a tangled web of trauma. Beginning with Columbus's 1492 arrival in the Americas, early European immigrants perpetrated genocide and forced removal on indigenous people who had lived here for centuries. In 1620, the Pilgrims landed at Plymouth and proceeded to assert control over lands and people. By the conclusion of King Philip's War in 1676, traditional indigenous life throughout New England was virtually exterminated.

Between 1619 and 1807, 12.5 million people were stolen from their homes in Africa and shipped to the so-called "New World." Almost two million perished during the horrible Middle Passage, while the surviving 10.7 million were taken in chains to North and South America and the Caribbean.[6] Between three hundred and four hundred thousand arrived in North America, in what is now the United States. By 1807, 80 percent of all people "who came from the Old World to the New had come from Africa, not Europe; chained in the belly of a ship, not free on its deck."[7] In 1865, four million enslaved people were emancipated, and six hundred thousand soldiers lay dead as a result of the Civil War.

After 1865, a century-long period of government-sanctioned discrimination, known as Jim Crow, ensued. Formerly enslaved people were subjected to lynching, forced displacement, convict-leasing, financial insecurity, social instability, medical experimentation, voter suppression, and sundown laws. This discrimination was designed to keep people of African descent permanently disenfranchised, disadvantaged, and living in fear, and it resulted in collective, cumulative, systemic, and structural trauma.

With the passage of the Civil and Voting Rights Acts in the 1960s, Jim Crow ended, but racial oppression did not. Michelle Alexander, in *The New Jim Crow*, demonstrates how the subsequent war on drugs disproportionately targeted black men and decimated

15

communities of color. The US criminal justice system worked to maintain racial control and disparity.

Today, white people and people of color fall on opposite ends of virtually all measurable social indicators, from infant mortality to poverty, unemployment, wealth, incarceration rates, education, housing, and health care. The cumulative effects of America's past are a compilation of historic traumatic wounds passed down through generations.

Get Over It
by Sharon Leslie Morgan

I am stoic and do not become destabilized when a crisis occurs. When, as a teen, my grandmother died in front of me and I was abandoned by the man who got me pregnant, I carried on. When my son was almost beaten to death by policemen, I took them to court. When robbers held me captive at gunpoint, I plotted my escape. I am proud of my resilience but sad about how I came to be this way.

My *small* personal experiences over a *brief* lifetime are *nothing* compared to what my ancestors endured for *centuries*. I have more than ten generations of trauma to overcome. White men enslaved my ancestors, sired children with the women without consent, profited from their financial value as commodities, participated as soldiers in a war to preserve slavery, terrorized them during 100 years of Jim Crow, and continue to disrespect and devalue our humanity and incarcerate and kill us in record numbers.

I will never fully know "from whence I came" since I can only go back to 1820, the year my earliest known enslaved ancestress was born. I will never know the names of her parents, siblings, and other children she likely had prior to Emancipation. Forever lost are the names of numerous white men who forced themselves onto my family tree through rape. My inability to name names contributes to the trauma.

I know the trauma of those I can name. Baby Rhoda Reeves was almost killed by the enraged wife of her white father. Owen Gavin committed suicide after being forced to watch the rape of his wife and daughter by "night riders." Samuel Nicholson and his sons were forced to sharecrop for their former owner. Henry Nicholson was lynched—for what?!! My mother was fired from a job when her employer realized she was not white. Her white mother was disowned by her family when she married a black man. And that's the *short* list of what needs healing for *one* family!

My ancestors somehow survived and became part of a chain (pun intended) that led to me—a socially conscious, twenty-first-century person who wants nothing more than to "get over it." I don't want the past to define the future prospects of my grandchildren and their children. As Alice Walker says, "Healing begins where the wound was made." Let's start there and pray for enlightenment.

Epigenetics

A word about passing traumatic wounds to future generations. Epigenetics is the study of mechanisms that switch various genes on or off without changing the underlying DNA. These epigenetic switches are involved in virtually all aspects of life and are heritable, thus affecting future generations. They influence health and disease, as well as emotional and psychological responses to events and situations. Epigenetic research suggests that racial prejudice, rooted in our brains long ago, is passed down through generations and continues to influence our instincts today. It is also believed that epigenetic effects occur in the womb and throughout our lives—and, most importantly, epigenetic changes may be reversed through the choices we make and environmental exposures.

Though traumatic wounds carried by people of color may be more obvious and easier to identify, what are the wounds carried by white people, descendants of enslavers and inheritors of the privileges and advantages that come with having white/light skin pigmentation? What wounds need addressing that come through guilt and shame, whether inherited or experienced in the present or through isolation and separation resulting from the legacy and aftermath of slavery?

The wounds inherited by white people are different, of course, but have nonetheless led to generations of woundedness. Harriet Jacobs, whose 1861 memoir recounts her experiences as a slave, writes: "I can testify, from my own experience and observation, that slavery is a curse to the whites as well as the blacks. It makes the white fathers cruel and sensual; the sons violent and licentious; it contaminates the daughters, and makes the wives wretched."[8] This trauma, and its impact today, also requires acknowledgment and healing.

As Adam Rutherford points out in *A Brief History of Everyone Who Ever Lived: The Human Story Retold Through Our Genes*, ". . . the world in which we live is shaped by us, by our practices and our culture, by our very existence, and our DNA respond to that in turn. Genes change culture, culture changes genes."[9]

Traumatic wounds cause severe harm to individuals, communities, and society, and they can be passed down to future generations. Yet we don't tend to talk about it much. Understanding trauma, becoming trauma-aware, and talking about trauma is fundamental to racial healing. This requires that we recognize and acknowledge any traumatic wounds we carry, the trauma others experience, and how trauma plays out in society (which we'll discuss more in subsequent chapters). All this is the first step toward racial healing.

3.
Restorative Justice

"Anti-black racism is in the culture. It's in our laws, in our advertisements, in our friendships, in our segregated cities, in our schools, in our Congress, in our scientific experiments, in our language, on the Internet, in our bodies no matter our race, in our communities, and, perhaps most devastatingly, in our justice system."[1]

—Claudia Rankine

The need for racial healing stems from the harms and historical trauma of slavery, Jim Crow, and other forms of racial injustice and inequity that continue today. The natural and reasonable response to these harms is to seek justice. As broadly understood and practiced in the United States, justice is "retributive" and often has little to do with healing. Whether in the criminal justice system, schools, or even families, when harm is committed, Howard Zehr suggests that we typically ask three questions in the search for justice:

1. What laws have been broken?
2. Who did it?
3. What do they deserve?[2]

This approach often feels justified: people believe that "reform" can come through punishment. But does locking away or shaming people who have harmed others ever truly result in reform or healing? The historic, traumatic racial wounds, and those that continue to be inflicted today, were and are horrific and mind-boggling. To heal such deep, systemic, and ongoing wounds requires accountability, justice, and repair.

Restorative justice is an alternative approach to retributive justice. It also offers philosophical and practical ways to address the harms of racial injustice and inequity. Indeed, restorative justice work *is* the work of racial healing. This is not a new approach; it has been lived throughout many communities across centuries, although it is known by different names, such as Gacaca in Rwanda and the Palava Huts in Liberia. Each process seeks to respond to harm in the community and move toward healing and reconciliation through dialogue and various forms of accountability. These approaches have been used around dinner tables and in religious gatherings and community ceremonies. When we create time to listen and hear each other, we move closer to one another.

Restorative Justice

Restorative justice (RJ) operates with additional and different intentions than the contemporary retributive justice system, which focuses on individual rights, individual justice, and punishment. Restorative justice seeks to identify and attend to the needs

21

and obligations of all who have been affected by the harm—i.e., both the offending and victimized individuals and communities—in order to move toward greater accountability and healing for everyone. Zehr offers three different questions that guide this form of justice (we paraphrase).[3]

1. Who has been harmed? (Including family and friends of those harmed and the perpetrator(s) of harm, bystanders, witnesses, responders, counselors, nurses, etc.)
2. What are the resulting needs of everyone who has been impacted?
3. Who has an obligation, or a role to play, to address those needs, repair the harm to the degree possible, and restore harmed relationships?

Restorative justice is community-centered, and where individual obligations are highlighted, it is in connection with obligations to relationships and the community. Because of this relational focus, restorative justice often brings together those who have been harmed and those who have committed harm to work toward healing, to the degree possible. It also includes affected community voices that have been plagued with the residue of the harm, expanding the realm of stakeholders and bringing a public element to the concept of justice.

We contend that a restorative approach to justice should be the standard by which we approach all sorts of harms, including racial harms. Practically speaking, restorative justice is harder work, and takes more time, than retributive justice. But the chance for healing and transformation for all is dramatically increased.

A common misconception about restorative justice is that it does not address the root causes of harm or hold offenders sufficiently accountable. When this is the case, restorative justice principles and practices are not being used properly. All harm, including the committing of harm, signifies broken relationships and woundedness on the part of all who are impacted, including the offender. Repair requires engagement and leaning into the harm in healthy ways, which means attending to causes.

Think about retributive justice for a moment. When someone is charged with a crime, it is "the state" (not the person or community who was harmed) versus the person who committed the harm. People are seen as either victims or offenders. Justice occurs behind closed doors. There is a desire for quick fixes (e.g., incarceration and fines), which invariably compound harm on the part of the victim and the offender. True healing and transformation are rarely achieved for either. Indeed, there are circumstances in which incarceration and separation from the community are appropriate. Yet there are many situations in which restorative practices would yield better results.

To understand the applicability of RJ principles to racial healing, it is important to understand the three core concepts.[4] First, RJ focuses on the harm(s) done to those who have been victimized, to those who have caused the harm, and to the community. It seeks to repair relationships to the degree possible for all who have been impacted. Second, harms result in obligations. Thus, the emphasis in RJ practices is on accountability and responsibility. Third, RJ promotes connection and engagement. Everyone impacted by the harm has a seat at the table and a role to play in deciding what justice and healing require. A restorative lens seeks to prioritize relationships while healing the harm and addressing the root causes. We can talk about the hard stuff and still maintain relationships.

Restorative Justice and Systems

Harm is a violation that can be committed by individuals as well as by systems. This includes the systemic, structural, and institutional racism evidenced by policies and practices that advantage white people and disadvantage people of color in areas such as economic well-being, educational achievement, housing security, health and health care, and treatment by the justice system. When used in racial healing, restorative justice seeks to address both the actions of individuals and the systems that perpetuate institutional harm. This requires an examination of the present-day ripples from the historic harm of slavery, which is perpetuated most clearly in our criminal justice and educational systems.

Black people are disproportionately entangled in and affected by involvement in the criminal justice system, especially as it relates to the mythology of "black-on-black crime" and mass incarceration. The myth of black-on-black crime perpetuates the existing narrative that black people are deviant and prone to violence and that the violence they experience at the hands of the state (i.e., police and courts) is insignificant compared to what happens in predominantly black communities. This belief ignores the fullness of the black experience and fails to name the historical and generational trauma that stems from institutional racism. This subconscious belief becomes dangerous when left unexamined. The story is not about reality but rather a false history maintained through structural and institutional racism.

The truth is that most people affected by crime are victimized by people of their same race; black people *and* white people. For the most part, poor people commit the most crime. Bureau of Justice statistics show the rate of violence is actually higher among poor white people in urban areas.[5] The real conversation should be around poverty.

The conversation should then shift to focus on why black people are treated more harshly within the criminal justice system than white people. For instance, black people make up roughly 14 percent of the US population, but 34 percent of those incarcerated. Black people are incarcerated at more than five times the rate of white people. Black and white people use illegal drugs at similar rates, but black people are imprisoned on drug charges almost six times as much as white people.[6]

This is not simply about discrimination but about the way that multiple forms of oppression and power affect black bodies. A key difference between retributive and restorative justice is that with the retributive approach, the "offender" is typically considered "the other," and the focus is on separation and locking them up. They disappear. They become nobody. A restorative approach focuses on community and our interconnectedness and shared experience and recognizes that racism is deeply tied to other forms of separation (e.g., gender, class, and religion). As Marc Lamont Hill says, "While Nobodyness is strongly tethered to race, it cannot be divorced from other forms of social injustice. Instead, it must be understood through the lens of 'intersectionality,' the ways that multiple forms of oppression operate simultaneously against the vulnerable. It would be impossible to examine the 2015 killing of Mya Hall by National Security Agency police without understanding how sexism and transphobia conspire with structural racism to endanger Black trans bodies. We cannot make sense of Sandra Bland's tragic death without recognizing the impact of gender and poverty in shaping the current carceral state. To understand the complexity of oppression, we must avoid simple solutions and singular answers."[7] A restorative approach acknowledges this intersectionality.

Racial inequality also plagues education disciplinary systems. According to a 2014 report by the US Department of Education's Office for Civil Rights, black students account for roughly 18 percent of pre-K enrollment in the United States, yet they accounted for 48 percent of preschoolers with multiple out-of-school suspensions. Black students were expelled at three times the rate of white students. American Indian and Native Alaskan girls were suspended at higher rates than white boys or girls.[8]

Restorative justice offers a way to address the systemic roots of these racial disparities in the education system, as well as in the criminal justice system. For instance, restorative practices in schools have been found to reduce racial disparities. Restorative Justice for Oakland Youth (RJOY) works for transformational change within the education system by using "restorative approaches that actively engage families, communities, and systems to repair harm and

26

prevent re-offending. RJOY focuses on reducing racial disparities and public costs associated with high rates of incarceration, suspension, and expulsion."[9] RJOY provides education, training, and technical assistance as well as demonstration programs with school, community, juvenile justice, and research partners.

RJOY's city-funded West Oakland Middle School pilot project eliminated violence and expulsions, reducing suspension rates by 87 percent. Within a year, nearly twenty Oakland school principals requested training to launch programs at their sites. To date, RJOY has served over 1,000 youth in Oakland's schools.

Caution is warranted, however. It is not enough to just *do* restorative justice; there must be an awareness of racism and power imbalances that exist within institutions and institutional structures. Without an approach that engages on every level, restorative practices (such as circle processes, discussed in a later chapter) can serve as a tool of punishment rather than a healing and accountability process. For instance, a circle can be designed that doesn't include the voices of the community or the young person. Circle process doesn't eliminate bias and racial inequity; it provides a way to investigate them. The potential exists for the process to be used to do *to*, instead of *with*, young people.

Anita Wadhwa, an educationally based restorative justice practitioner, contends that "Restorative practitioners aiming to reduce racial disparities in school discipline must be familiar with the institutions in which they are operating to create lasting, system-wide change. In understanding the historic antecedents to the racial discipline gap, they may be able to

27

craft a new paradigm of addressing harm that can disrupt racialized disciplinary practices in schools."[10] In other words, practitioners must become familiar with the historical impacts of racially biased school discipline to best serve and meet the needs of young people. The same can be said for using restorative justice practices in the criminal justice system.

The Witnesses
by Cassandra Lane

Dear Great-Grandma Mary,
When I was a little girl playing the hangman game, I didn't yet know that someone in our bloodline had been lynched. By the time I left for college, I knew this ugly part of our family's history: my paternal great-grandfather, your first love, Burt, had been lynched.

I have been on a quest to explore how the racist slaughtering of Burt has impacted our family—physically, mentally, spiritually, economically—across generations. I do not know if I would have your blessings in this quest. Because you are my oldest and most visceral connection to our past, I cling to my childhood memory of you in your nineties, sitting on our porch, spitting snuff into a jar as you shooed away some ghost. "Get on away from here, you haint," you would say. "Get on away from here. Ain't nobody studying you." But my eyes and ears and skin were studying you. Sense recordings.

You, what was done to you and how you chose to deal with life, preprogrammed me. The coding was already set, wasn't it, even for you? All I am trying to do is decipher the calculations, so that I can keep what worked well for us and disconnect that which caused us to malfunction.

* * *

I am preparing to take a DNA test to see what can be determined beyond you, my great-grand . . . were your parents or grandparents enslaved? Part of me rails against ordering this test. Why must I pay to attempt to uncover what was stolen from us? And what if my fingers come up empty or worse, with some thin and cloudy connection that holds no real clue to who we are? Smoke and shadow. Things that cannot be held or buried. Still, I will take the test to uncover what stories await inside our complicated network of DNA.

Physically, I will return to the beginning of you and Burt, to Holmesville, Mississippi, which is now a ghost town. If I see no live human bodies, I know the trees will still be there—the dirt, the grass, the remains underneath. And I will be listening for their whispers of truth.

What are we restoring? We are restoring the inherent and deserved dignity of all. Some may feel this notion of dignity fails to acknowledge the deep historical harms of slavery, Jim Crow, and racism. However, it creates the possibility for deeper and radically honest conversations that are steeped in dignity. Donna Hicks asserts that "dignity is different from respect. Dignity is a birthright. We have little trouble seeing this when a child is born; there is no question about children's value and worth. If only we could hold onto this truth about human beings as they grow into adults, if only we could continue to *feel* their value, then it would be so much easier to treat them well and keep them safe from harm. Treating others with dignity, then, becomes the baseline for our interactions. We must treat others as if they matter, as if they are worthy of care and attention."[11] By adopting restorative justice theory and practices, we move toward effectively addressing historic and present-day traumatic racial wounds and restoring the dignity of all of us.

4.
Uncovering History

"There is not a country in world history in which racism has been more important, for so long a time, as the United States. And the problem of 'the color line,' as W. E. B. DuBois put it, is still with us."[1]
—Howard Zinn

Racial transformation, and approaching all aspects of our lives through an anti-racist and anti-oppression lens, rests on four equally important and interconnected pillars: uncovering history, making connections, working toward healing, and taking action. Trauma awareness and restorative justice further support each of these pillars This chapter focuses on the first pillar: uncovering history.

Uncovering history helps highlight the historic wounds that need healing and that continue to be perpetuated across generations. Woundedness from racism resides within individuals. However, the racist systems and structures at the core of American society, which affect everyone, are even more important. Racial disparities, such as those discussed in the previous chapter, represent symptoms of these collective wounds.

Many parts of US history, especially the unsavory and damaging parts, have often been systematically and purposefully buried. While doing so is understandable, hiding the shameful truths of history paints a false and incomplete picture of who we are today and where we came from. To heal wounds of racism, we must see racism for what it is and understand its causes, origin, development, and subsequent impact. This understanding emerges through research, acknowledgment, and the open and honest sharing of personal, family, community, and national histories of race. Uncovering and acknowledging the full history of racism in the United States provides the foundation for a new or increased understanding of the present-day consequences of the traumatic wounds festering from the legacy and aftermath of slavery. Two well-known stories from twentieth-century US history—*Brown v. Board of Education* and the GI Bill—exemplify how an incomplete picture alters the understanding of the impact of critical events and decisions.

Brown v. Board of Education

Students in the United States are taught about *Brown v. Board of Education*, the landmark 1954 case in which the Supreme Court unanimously declared state laws establishing separate public schools for black and white students to be unconstitutional and "inherently unequal." The decision effectively overturned *Plessy v. Ferguson*, the 1896 decision that allowed state-sponsored segregation in public education. *Brown v. Board of Education* is considered a major victory of the civil rights movement.

However . . .

The decision was implemented slowly across the United States, with mixed results. Laws were not applied universally, and in many areas, white people moved to the suburbs, creating all-white enclaves and schools. In Detroit, Michigan, for instance, the students are almost all people of color. In Grosse Pointe, a city next to Detroit, the students are almost all white. Further, the decision intended to integrate students but not teachers. In many cases, black schools were simply closed, black children were integrated into formerly all-white schools, and black teachers were fired. In 1954, there were approximately 82,000 African American teachers in the South. By 1964, about half had been fired.

Without black teachers, black students were left without important role models, which carries particular significance given that schools are places where students learn about authority, social power, and opportunity. Reflecting on her experiences of desegregation in Kentucky, bell hooks writes, "We black kids had been angry that we had to leave our beloved all-black high school, Crispus Attucks, and be bussed halfway cross town to integrate white schools. We had to make the journey and we had to give up the familiar and enter a world that seemed cold and strange, not our world, not our school. We were certainly on the margins, no longer the center, and it hurt."[2]

When authority, power, and opportunity rest almost exclusively with white people, black students feel the impact. Research shows, for instance, that black students who have a black teacher achieve higher test scores, behave differently, and experience fewer suspensions than when they have a white teacher. A recent study found that "having even one Black teacher between the third and fifth grade reduced the chance [that] an African American boy would later drop out of high school. By how much? By 39 percent. One Black teacher." The researchers concluded, "To this day, the ranks of Black teachers in the United States have not recovered from the humiliations and mass firings of the 1950s and 60s. As a percentage, there are far fewer Black teachers than there are Black students and when you think back to studies on how important Black teachers are for the performance of Black students, that's a tragedy."[3]

Is there any surprise there are racial disparities? The system creates and sustains them.

The GI Bill of Rights

The Selective Service Readjustment Act, popularly known as the GI Bill of Rights, had a greater impact on changing the United States than any other New Deal initiative. Between 1944 and 1971, support for returning soldiers totaled more than $95 billion. By 1948, the Veterans Administration employed 17 percent of the federal workforce, and GI Bill spending represented 15 percent of the federal budget. Millions of returning veterans were able to buy homes, attend college, start businesses, and find jobs.

However . . .

The GI Bill was designed to accommodate existing Jim Crow laws in the South. In the North and West, it was applied in ways that benefited white veterans far more than black veterans. The GI Bill, in fact, widened the racial gap in the United States.

White veterans secured financial advantages related to housing that literally created the almost all-white suburbs outside the nation's cities. Black veterans were routinely denied home loans promised in the bill. In 1947, of the more than 3,000 VA-guaranteed loans that were distributed in Mississippi, exactly two went to black veterans. Such disparities were not limited to the South. In the suburbs in New York and northern New Jersey, fewer than 100 non-white borrowers received one of the 67,000 mortgages insured by the GI Bill. Nearly five million new homes were paid for by VA loans, which were offered at modest rates—and often with down payments waived— almost exclusively to white veterans. In California, 6 percent of home mortgages were insured by the federal government in 1936. By 1950, that percentage ballooned to fully half, creating economic security for the growing, and largely white, middle class.

The gap in education widened, thus perpetuating the disparities created by the implementation of *Brown v. Board of Education*. Quotas and selectivity severely restricted black veterans' access to colleges outside the South. In 1946, the University of Pennsylvania had nine thousand students enrolled. Forty-six were black. Insufficient support for black colleges in the South left them unable to accommodate most eligible black veterans.[4]

Think of the consequences over time. Those who own homes benefit from the equity generated by increased value, and subsequent generations inherit the financial gains. Those with higher-skilled, better-paying jobs enter higher income levels and more exclusive social classes. The impact extends to education, given that public schools are largely funded by property taxes. All-white suburbs with high property values and substantial tax revenues mean better-funded schools in the suburbs, compared to inner cities. These institutional policies resulted in a stark increase in racial disparities and allowed trauma to permeate through communities. They gave birth to various forms of institutional racism that became harder to name and identify.

Lynching

Institutional policies are not limited to written legislation; they exist in unwritten rules that maintain oppression through the norming of racist ideologies and social behaviors. Lynching, a strategic form of terror, illustrates deeply rooted ideologies and behaviors that require unveiling and acknowledgment. The Equal Justice Initiative (EJI) describes lynching as "racial terror" and states that "[t]he geographic, political, economic, and social consequences of decades of terror lynchings can still be seen in many communities today and the damage created by lynching needs to be confronted and discussed. Only then can we meaningfully address the contemporary problems that are lynching's legacy."[5]

Lynching served as a hyper-public and deadly form of violence that sent a clear message to black people about the supremacy of whiteness. These terrorist acts confirmed the extreme violence forced upon black people that existed in other forms of structural and social limitations. For example, the Civil Rights Act of 1964 called for protection against discrimination in public facilities and institutions, but white businesses and predominantly white communities refused to serve black customers, sell homes to black families, or allow their children to attend school with black children. This denial of dignity is also a form of violence and places a low value on the life of black people and other people of color. This kind of violence moves beyond the symbolism of a noose and highlights the direct use of state-sponsored, -supported, and sometimes -inflicted violence against black bodies. One can argue that the modern-day terrorism of police violence and the over-militarization of black, brown, and immigrant communities directly reflects the United States' history of lynching and failure to protect the rights of marginalized peoples. Just as lynching was a public expression of other forms of hidden structural violence, these new forms of terrorism function as structural and social discrimination and violence and require uncovering.

State, Local, and Personal History

Stories of discrimination and violence exist in virtually every state and community. The work of racial healing requires researching the history of racism and white supremacy where you live.

Researching and developing a "community history of race" for your town, county, or state helps uncover your local history. Perhaps you live in a former "Sundown Town," one of thousands that excluded African Americans and other minority groups after sundown. Perhaps your community practiced "redlining," where real estate agents steered non-white customers away from certain neighborhoods and toward others. Maybe community black people could not get insured loans from the Federal Housing Administration (a regular occurrence until the late 1960s). Why does your town "look" the way it does? Who lives where? Do you have "the other side of the tracks"? People so often ignore or excuse historic harms committed in their community, taking resulting present-day circumstances for granted. *It's just the way things are* or *always have been*. The impact of taking present circumstances for granted can be deeply racist and harmful, in your community, today.

As Ibram X. Kendi wrote in *Stamped from the Beginning,* "There was nothing simple or straightforward or predictable about racist ideas, and thus their history. Frankly speaking, for generations of Americans, racist ideas have been their common sense. The simple logic of racist ideas has manipulated millions over the years, muffling the more complex antiracist reality again and again."[6] What is your "common sense"? What is *your* personal history? Knowing your own history—your ancestry and your genealogy—facilitates understanding how and why you ended up where you live and to whom you are related. It un-muffles *"the more complex antiracist reality"* and uncovers why you believe what you believe and why you respond as you do with issues of race.

When we know ourselves better and understand just how deeply interconnected we all are, the desire to heal racial wounds and overcome that which divides us can take on increased importance and urgency.

My Grandmother's Boxes
by Leslie Stainton

Like many descendants of slaveholders, I was taught that my ancestors had suffered terribly after the Civil War and to admire them for their strength and courage, without question. My grandmother—the primary source of this information—said nothing about the fact that for nearly fifty years those same ancestors had bought, sold, hunted, and abused scores of human beings. "There are things we don't talk about," my grandmother said whenever I asked about the war.

This same grandmother amassed boxes of family documents and damning records that told the truth. I recently opened the ancestral boxes and began reading. Inside, I found letters telling my great-great-great-grandfather how to feed the enslaved people on his plantation. "It will be dangerous to feed the negroes too early on new corn until it is dry." I found letters describing the escape, in 1862, by nearly two dozen enslaved people from my family. "Independent of the loss," one of my ancestors wrote, "the trust betrayed causes many a pang." I found an oral history describing the purchase, in 1858, by my great-great-great-grandfather, of an enslaved African man from the illicit slave ship *The Wanderer* and his decision to rent the man to fellow slaveholders "as a producer of children for $100 a day."

If my grandmother's boxes held facts like this, what else was out there? In my research, I found records that detailed how family members mortgaged and bequeathed human beings and fathered mixed-race babies with enslaved women. I discovered census records listing the hundreds of human beings my ancestors professed to own and ads seeking to purchase humans and offering rewards for the capture of runaway enslaved people.

In time, I met descendants of people my ancestors enslaved. I shared with them copies of the letters describing how *their* ancestors had escaped from my family. To me, these courageous African Americans were the heroes of our collective story— for at the height of the war, they had commandeered a boat and sailed past Confederate troops into open sea to realize their dreams of freedom. One of the descendants told me how proud she was to learn their story. "This is something we will truly cherish."

I knew then why I had opened my grandmother's boxes—why everyone who shares in this difficult history needs to do what we can to uncover it.

5.
Making
Connections

"Relationships are primary. All else is derivative."

Rev. Ron David, MD, wrote the words above on a chalkboard in a classroom at the John F. Kennedy School of Government, where he taught leadership classes for senior executives in state and local government. He said that nothing matters more to us as human beings than to be in a relationship, for the sake of being in a relationship. We want to be in love, love others, and be loved by others.

A key task in racial healing is to examine the underlying damage to relationships and repair them. History can be (and certainly has been) remembered and presented in ways that continue to hurt and divide, thus the need to re-explore and uncover history and understand the impact of past events on people then and now. Racial healing relies on then building relationships with people we have thought of as the "other," listening to their stories, and developing our capacity for compassion and empathy in the service of healing.

Connecting with Your Own Story

We are each complex human beings, shaped by a wide variety of experiences, memories, and inheritances. We have been taught and conditioned about how to perceive race—our own, and that of others. Our thoughts create our reality and shape our perceptions and beliefs, which in turn influence our emotions, decisions, and actions. The first step to racial healing is to connect with our own stories of race, what we have been taught, and what we believe to be true. Richard Stone points out "that before we can effectively repair the world, we must look inward, searching for wholeness among all the fractured parts."[1] Without understanding our own stories, we will pass the harm embedded in our stories, and our DNA, along to future generations. Our interactions with others will not support healing and will, even with good intentions, perpetuate woundedness.

This inward look entails excavating and examining our own story, as well as those of our families and nation, and the place where we reside within these stories and racial woundedness. Ask yourself some questions:

- What do I believe has been the impact, on different people from different backgrounds, of living in a society built by the stolen labor of enslaved people on land stolen from indigenous people?
- If my family was in North America during the time of enslavement, how does it feel to

be associated with the oppressors? How does it feel to be associated with oppressors if my family was *not* in North America then?

- If my family was in North America during the time of enslavement, how does it feel to be associated with people who were oppressed? How does it feel to be associated with people who were oppressed if my family was *not* here then?

- What does this mean for me if I don't self-identify as African American or European American? Are there other historical and current injustices that have affected my life?

- What forms of race-based trauma, and other forms of trauma, have been experienced by me or my people/ancestors? What forms of race-based trauma, and other forms of trauma, can I imagine have been experienced by people with different backgrounds than mine?

- How did I learn about race and racial divisions?

- How has what I have learned affected my life and how I see people?

A key factor in knowing ourselves and our stories is understanding our own unconscious biases. We all carry biases, prejudices, stereotypes, and preconceived notions about other people, institutions, and situations we encounter daily. Like trauma, such notions typically operate at the level of instinct, deeply rooted in our "lizard" brains. Transforming our stories relies on our awareness, acknowledgment, and confrontation of unconscious biases that influence our thoughts, words, and actions in ways that cause harm. One good resource is free and available online: Project Implicit and the Implicit Association Tests (IAT), which measure attitudes and beliefs in a variety of areas through simple and fun tests.[2]

With sufficient reflection into your own story and unconscious biases, you will increase your understanding of what you do and don't believe about issues of race and why. You likely will move beyond "that's the way it was/is" thinking and discover that you can undo old habits and shift your beliefs and use them in the service of racial healing and transformation. You may well experience increased empathy and a new common humanity with people whose lives and histories are different from yours. You will hopefully develop an interest and willingness to hear other people's stories.

Sharing Our Stories and Listening to Others

Sharing our stories with each other is pretty much the only way to develop meaningful relationships. Richard Stone continues: "[T]elling a story, especially about ourselves, may be one of the most personal and intimate things we can do. Through storytelling, we can come to know who we are in new and unforeseen ways. We can also reveal to others what is deepest in our hearts, in the process, building bridges. The very act of sharing a story with another human being contradicts the extreme isolation that characterizes so many of our lives. As such, storytelling carries within it the seeds of community. And, because stories take time and patience, they serve as potent antidotes to a modern society's preoccupation with technology and speed."[3]

To understand each other and experience mutual and deep relationships, we must truly and deeply hear each other's stories. Through sharing stories about the legacy and aftermath of slavery, we create a new, shared story—and a shared identity as a nation—that includes the (hi)stories and experiences of trauma of all groups. Storytelling makes it possible to confront and overcome white supremacy, separation, and hierarchies of human value and develop authentic, accountable, and healthy relationships from which to plan collective actions to bridge divides and transform our communities. The mutuality of these relationships ensures that those actions result from the input of people from all sides of racial divides. Racial healing depends on everyone joining together in the work.

Sharing and listening to stories can be emotional and difficult. We may discover that much of what we learned in history class was mis-taught, with key factors glossed over or deliberately hidden. This discovery can be deep and transformative. Many people take listening for granted and find it challenging to listen to and communicate with others respectfully, without fear of being interrupted, belittled, or condemned. If one does not exhibit good listening skills, others will be reluctant to share their personal and painful stories. Indeed, making connections requires courage and likely some degree of discomfort. The next chapter explores a process that creates an environment to support storytelling and relationship building.

The Gordon
by Danita Rountree Green

I don't remember when she walked into the museum, but I was suddenly aware of the white woman standing a few feet away, intensely looking at the painting. She wrapped herself in her own embrace, arms crossed, her fingers digging into her shoulders, silently weeping.

"Looking at *Gordon* will do that to you," I said.

"What?"

"*Gordon: The Scourged Back*. That's the name of this piece," I offered. We stood together taking in the iconic image of a slave, his back whipped mercilessly, the grotesque lacerations revealed his horrific trauma and that of his generations.

"It's painful to behold," she said, sniffling.

Yeah, I thought to myself, *and indicative of what I experience as a black woman raising another generation of black folks. I bear my own invisible scars, lady.*

The white woman looked at me, waiting for my interpretation of the painting. And then it happened. She threw herself into my arms, crying uncontrollably.

"I'm sorry," she blurted.

"Sorry for *what?*" I asked.

"Sorry for it all!" she moaned. "How you people have suffered for all of these years!"

I tried my best to comfort the woman as she first lamented and then confessed, telling me about her slave-holding family. She told me about the fortune that her ancestors amassed and the tremendous privilege she had experienced in her lifetime, "all because of the slaves we owned in Virginia." Cringing, all I could think about was how different this woman's life had been from mine, possibly due to the enslavement of my ancestors. "I'm so sorry," she repeated, before releasing me and hurrying away.

I stood there alone in front of *The Gordon*, tempted to touch where the lash had been. I closed my eyes and became one with what he had survived. *Perseverance. Resilience. I am alive because you lived!* "Thank you," I said out loud.

I casually mentioned my experience in the museum to my friend, Martha. "This crazy white woman actually cried," I said. Silent, Martha's eyes filled with the same burden as the woman in the museum. We had been friends long enough for me to actually forget how *white* she was. I reached for her hand, not because I understood her pain but to acknowledge that she was in pain, and that the trauma she experienced, growing up white, was somehow mine, too.

Next Steps

Racial healing calls us to be aware of our stories of race and those of others. It calls us to acknowledge the trauma of individuals that affects generations, challenges communities, and becomes woven into the fabric of history. The scars run deep for those who received the bite of the lash and those who held the whip. However, when we tell our stories, build relationships, stand together, and acknowledge our past—our *Gordon*—we can dismantle the fear and the pain. Ultimately, it is the recognition and embracing of our shared humanity—our universal interconnectedness—that will break down walls that separate people, improve our compassion and empathy with each other, and lead to the possibility of healing and transformation.

Even if you do not feel completely confident, we invite you to go for it. Start a conversation. Talk to family, friends, or colleagues. Invite friends to watch a relevant film and talk about it after. Suggest a book for your reading group to discuss (see our list of recommendations). Participate in a workshop on confronting racism. Join a group in your community already working on these issues. Help start just such a group.[4] Ask questions. Listen.

6.
Circles, Touchstones, and Values

"In many of my talks to young people, to women, to peace activists, etc., I advocate that in these times of planetary disasters and instability people everywhere should gather together in circles of friends, in each other's homes, on a regular basis, to talk through the fears and challenges with which we, as a world, are faced: more frightening events at this time than at any period in human history. It is time to circle, I advise, with the hope that eventually our diverse circles will engage each other, merge, and organically transform the earth."[1]

—Alice Walker

Racial healing is deeply complex and emotional work. How do we best embrace the opportunity to show up for this journey—to share our stories, listen to others' experiences, speak to what we have learned, and show what we can do to support racial transformation? We do so together in community or, as Alice Walker wrote, in "circle."

Circles are an intentionally created dialogue method where the gathering space is designed to encourage storytelling and relationship building; it is where participants feel brave, committed, and safe enough to stay with the dialogue when things get difficult. And with an issue like race, we can count on things getting difficult. This chapter introduces the circle process both as a path to accountability, repair, and transformation around issues of race and racial justice, and as a deliberate action we can take together in a community.

The Roots of Circles

The circle process is an ancient, indigenous tradition that creates space "to solve problems, support one another, and connect to one another."[2] Circles create space for restorative justice work: for breaking down barriers, deep listening, sharing stories, building trust, and peacebuilding. We can look to the traditions of the "medicine wheel" or "sacred hoop," taught by North and South American First Nation, indigenous, and aboriginal peoples, for understanding of the power of the circle process. All humans have basic needs in four broad areas: physical, mental, emotional, and spiritual. "From a Medicine Wheel perspective, we're not only matter or only mind, neither are we only emotions or even only spiritual beings. We are all these together—physical, mental, emotional, and spiritual. All four facets are essential to our existence, and they must be balanced for an activity to be successful or for a person, family, or community to be healthy."[3] Circles create this balance.

Too often, the "Western" approach elevates, or glorifies, the physical and mental aspects and diminishes, or even crushes, the spiritual and emotional aspects. How often do we hear "she's so emotional" or "he's so kumbaya" as negative or critical put-downs? Analyzing concepts mentally and applauding physical achievements are fine and good. Diminishing spiritual and emotional aspects of ourselves and others cuts us off from understanding ourselves and our relationships and interconnectedness with each other. Far too often, we feel emotionally and spiritually broken and hurt in our relationships. Being in circle offers the possibility of repairing what's broken and healing our emotions and spirits.

In circle, each person is invited to share their stories and to speak their truths in all four areas (physical, mental, emotional, and spiritual). Additionally, each person cannot assume their truth is the truth for others. The circle is different from any other spaces in which humans typically operate or interact. The space itself is set up to highlight the sacredness of what takes place within each of us along all four dimensions and moves us closer toward living with the fullness of what it means to be human. From the teachings of the Medicine Wheel, it is the balance of all four that allows for healing to occur.

The image on the following page (see Figure 2) represents the balance of four relational elements within the circle process: getting acquainted, building relationships, exploring issues, and making plans. Though not a direct or exclusive correlation, the physical and mental elements align primarily with the elements on

51

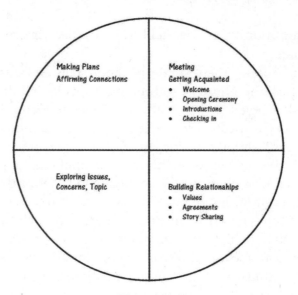

Figure 2.

the left side of the diagram, and the emotional and spiritual elements primarily with those on the right.

These four relational elements of the circle process support the creation of a brave/safe-enough space to lean into conflict and difficult conversations. The process begins on the upper right, with the meeting/getting acquainted elements, and moves clockwise around the circle. It is important to spend at least as much time on the right side of this image as the left. Without the right side, we get stuck on the left; we haven't built the trusting and authentic relationships necessary to effectively confront the issues. Spending literally half or more of our time on the work on the right side is what allows for effectiveness on the left side; we must build the relationships to confront the issues. The "action" that allows for success in exploring issues, making plans, and creating sustainable transformation is all on the right side of this illustration.

The "Act" of Being in Circle

The idea of encouraging conversations on race is sometimes criticized for being "too much talk" and "too little action." We disagree. Building authentic and accountable relationships and sharing our heart-felt stories with each other, with the goal of individual and collective healing, is the beginning of lasting transformation. Consequently, meeting regularly in circle is one of the best forms of action we know to offer the possibility of successful racial healing. This approach does not preclude actions such as marches, lobbying, petition signing, arguing, and changing laws to work toward healing. All are important tools for change. Unless we also transform hearts and minds, people will find ways to perpetuate harm, difference, and separation.

The act of being in circle contributes to transformation by creating space to understand people's varied experiences related to race, privilege, oppression, and social justice, especially as it relates to intersectionality and the social construction of race. As discussed in Chapter 3, intersectionality refers to patterns of oppression around race that are interrelated with and operate collectively alongside similar patterns based on gender, sexual orientation, class, disability, and age. For instance, the experiences of low-income white families may be similar in some ways to those of low-income black families and different in others. Thus, the intersectionality of race and class.

The social construction of "race" refers to the fact that "race" is not biological. People made it up within various contexts (legal, cultural, political, and economic) to create and define differences between white people and people of color; it is an artificial distinction to create different forms of superiority and dominance in some and inferiority and subordination in others. Adam Rutherford points out that "there are no essential genetic elements for any particular group of people who might be identified as a 'race.' As far as genetics is concerned, race does not exist."[4] It is from this social construction of race that the concept of "white privilege" derives.

"Privilege," says Franchesca Ramsey from MTV's *Decoded*, "is defined as a special right or advantage available only to a particular person or group of people. In the context of social inequality, it means that some groups of people are treated better than others based on their race, gender, class, sexuality, or physical ability." Mentioning "white privilege" often feels like casting blame. Challenging this notion, Ramsey continues: "Talking about privilege is not meant to make you feel guilty. Guilt isn't productive. Acknowledging it isn't about shame. It's about challenging the system that perpetuates inequality."[5]

The circle process challenges participants to see each other through an intersectional lens; to recognize that various patterns of oppression and privilege are hardwired into systems and structures of society and harm people in multiple ways, with varying degrees of intensity. In recognizing this, participants create a new image of themselves and the world that is different from the master narratives that highlight the accomplishments of white people and erase or ignore the accomplishments and struggles of people of color. The circle process does not seek to dismiss or excuse white privilege or the multiple ways in which white people contribute to cycles of violence and harm while benefiting from white privilege. To the contrary, effective circles will enlighten all participants about their privilege and accountability.

When practiced effectively, the circle humanizes everyone more fully. It moves away from the idea of people being the problem and to a place of seeing the problem as the problem. Dr. David Anderson Hooker explains: "For instance, as opposed to people being characterized as 'fearful of one another,' the context could be described as a place where 'fear shows up and people react differently' to the presence of fear. In the former description fear is identified as a condition of the people; in the latter instance fear is externalized as a character with its own role to play, actions, and motivations. When fear is its own character, other characters can react differently to it because it is not an essential part of their character. This externalizing process establishes a wider range of options for transforming the context."[6]

Within the context of this book, as opposed to people being characterized as "racist," the context could be described as a situation, event, or comment in which racism shows up. Calling someone a racist is unlikely to have any positive outcomes. Treating the problem as the problem, and noting the different ways in which white people or people of color are affected by—and respond to—the situation, event, or comment carries the potential for a more positive outcome.

Essential Elements of the Circle

The circle process provides equal opportunity for all participants to contribute and feel heard and valued by intentionally creating a relational space within which everyone has equal dignity and worth. This is not simply putting a bunch of chairs in a circle and talking. Deliberate and advanced preparation is critically important for success. We offer the following essential circle elements.

Sitting in a Circle

Circle work occurs by actually sitting in a circle so everyone can see everyone else, with no sides and no corners in which to hide. Participants are accountable to each other, face-to-face, where everyone can hear people's stories and witness nonverbal communication. Being in circle creates space to share deeply in different ways. The first step of sitting in circle begins the process of shifting embedded forms of communication rooted in power imbalances and a win-lose polarity that is often present in other facilitated processes. Circles, lived with intention and care, model the equality and interconnectedness necessary for difficult topics.

Circle Keeper

The role of the circle keeper is analogous to that of a monitor, not an enforcer. The keeper supports the group in building and sustaining a space where everyone feels welcome to speak from the heart and where individual and collective wisdom can emerge. In other processes, the facilitator holds tremendous power and decides who talks next. In the circle process, power is distributed equally through the use of a talking piece, and the keeper helps create and assure equality while exhibiting care, humility, and flexibility with the group. Keepers rarely intervene and do so only if group agreements or values are compromised; in such situations, the keeper takes care about how and where to use her or his voice.

Talking Piece

A talking piece is used to equalize the circle, reduce the control of the keeper (or anyone), and distribute that control equally among the participants. The implicit understanding is that everyone has important wisdom to share with the group. The talking piece is passed around the circle, in order, from person to person, giving each participant equal opportunity to share. Only the holder of the talking piece may speak and does so without being interrupted. Everyone else in the circle listens deeply to what the holder shares. Power is found in the listening because it challenges everyone to be present, not focused in the next moment or conversation to come. Each participant has the choice to pass rather than share. The quietest voice is not shamed or ignored in passing, while the loudest voice is not praised. Ideally, the talking piece will be an item that represents the topic of discussion or something relevant to the particular group. It is typically, but not always, selected by the keeper.

Centerpiece

Many circles include a centerpiece, or altar, at the center of the circle. A centerpiece can symbolize the importance of the gathering and create a focus for the circle. Initially, the keeper typically sets it up, though participants are often invited to bring an object representing some important aspect of their lives as a personal contribution to the centerpiece.

Some circles place a quilt or other woven cloths to represent the diverse pieces and people being drawn together into community and to symbolize the interconnectedness of circle participants. A candle may represent light, warmth, and transformation; a cup of water may suggest cleansing. Participants may ask ancestors to watch over the circles by writing their names on pieces of paper and placing them in the centerpiece. Various talking pieces that may be used during the circle can also be placed within the centerpiece.

Circle Process

Each circle may have a different purpose: to resolve conflicts, to connect with each other, to celebrate a person or group achievement, to support each other, to learn from and about each other, or to listen to and share specific stories. Each of these types of circle can be used for confronting issues connected to race. Even with different purposes, there are several standard components of the circle.

Introductions

The first time a group meets in circle, or whenever new participants join a group in a regularly scheduled circle process, introductions are important. People need to know who is in the room, of course, but introductions also set the tone for the circle and begin to show how this process is different from most other gatherings. Most importantly, in introductions, participants share who they are and why it matters to be in the circle; that is, why they are taking the time out of their lives to be there.

Touchstones and Values

A circle process begins with intentional commitment and consensus about how the conversation will be held through the development of shared touchstones and values. Values and touchstones are interconnected; touchstones are the values we agree to in action.

Touchstones are an established set of mutually agreed-upon principles that guide how participants will treat, and be with, each other. They aim to address participants' needs and expectations to feel safe enough to speak openly and honestly and help them to make more space for each other. There should not be too many nor should they be too rigid, lest they feel like a straitjacket. The touchstones are reminders of standards of behavior, not hard rules. They are a means to an end, a way toward relationship. If they become the end, they should be revisited.

The one essential touchstone is to honor the talking piece when it is being used. Other important agreements include respecting each other, speaking from your heart, maintaining confidentiality (depending on the purpose of each circle), and being aware of time (i.e., take the time you need to speak while respecting the needs of others). Other examples include:

- **Welcome others** and presume that you are welcomed.
- **Be 100 percent present.** Bring all of yourself to the experience, setting aside outside distractions.
- **Try it on.** Make an opening for new ideas by trying them on for size, getting to know them, and considering how they fit you.

- **Always by invitation.** You may be invited to share in pairs, in small groups, and in the large group, and *you* determine the extent to which you want to participate.
- **No fixing.** Participation is not about setting someone else straight, helping right another's wrong, or "correcting" what is perceived as broken or incorrect in another participant. The intention is that each participant will discover his or her own truths and what she/he may need to learn, change, or adapt. Others will undoubtedly experience change as well. The recognition here is that the only person any of us can truly change is our self.
- **Expect "non-closure."** Stay in the present and recognize that the dialogue will not get to the end of the road or the answer to injustice and oppression in one conversation or one day.[7]

Sometimes, the circle keeper(s) will hand out a list of sample or suggested touchstones at the beginning of a circle for consideration; other times, the group develops a list from scratch; or facilitators may use a combination of both approaches. Regardless of approach, keepers solicit participants' suggestions for any additions to the touchstones and reactions to any to which participants do not agree. The touchstone discussion concludes with a circle round in which all participants indicate their agreement to them.

Participants also develop consensus around shared values. Our values inform our choices, thoughts, actions, and words each day and reflect what is important to us. When groups identify shared values, cohesion results. Typically, values in circle after circle are universally similar—love, trust, compassion, and so on. Even so, each group needs to name them for themselves, so they own them. The values guide the conversations about harms, making it essential to write them down and make them visible, along with the touchstones, either in the centerpiece or some other display.

Undoubtedly, participants will learn a lot about themselves as they learn about each other through the process of creating the touchstones and values. Participants identify places where they do and do not have common ground, thus beginning the important work of building authentic and accountable relationships (the right side of the circle illustration) for the challenging conversations that directly confront systems and structures of racism, white supremacy, and the legacy of slavery (the left side of the circle illustration).

Safety
The centerpiece, keeper, talking piece, touchstones, and values all support the cultivation of a space that maximizes safety, but safety cannot be promised because we do not know what "safety" means to each person. So efforts are made to create a relational container that hopefully feels safe enough and where people will stay when it may not feel as safe.

Guiding Questions
The keeper carefully designs questions to inspire thoughtful conversation and encourages participants to dive deep into their perspectives and feelings about the topic under discussion. The keeper poses a question for each circle round and invites each participant to respond. They may begin with getting-acquainted

61

questions such as "How would your friends describe you?" Or, "If you could talk for an hour with someone who is no longer alive, who would it be, and why?" They may be questions about how we became who we are today, such as "Share an experience in which you did not fit in." Or, "Share an experience of crisis in your life where you discovered a power you didn't realize you had." Racial healing circles will obviously include questions essential to racial healing work, perhaps similar to those raised in Chapter 5: "What do you believe has been the impact, on different people from different backgrounds, of living in a society built by the stolen labor of enslaved people on land stolen from indigenous people?" "How does it feel to be associated with the oppressors, or with people who were oppressed?" "How did you learn about race and racial divisions?" Your group can develop questions relevant to your experiences and community.

Opening and Closing Ceremonies

Keepers use opening and closing ceremonies to signify the sacredness of the circle and help participants see themselves and each other in ways that are different from ordinary life. Effective openings invite participants to break free from the normal barriers that separate them from each other and to bring their full selves into the space. Effective closings acknowledge what the participants have done together, and their interconnectedness, as well as provide transitions back to normal life.

Opening ceremony examples to get you started include:

- Reciting a mantra or prayer
- Guided meditation

- Calling ancestors into the space: While gathered in circle, participants speak the name of a family member, friend, or person of significance they would like to call into the space. This ceremony acknowledges our interconnectedness with those who have come before. The name called is usually, but not always, someone who has passed on.
- Whose shoulders do you stand on? Who will be standing on your shoulders? On a rock or another object, participants write the initials of an elder upon whose shoulders they stand; someone from whom they've learned lessons or who they admire. On the other side of the object, participants write the initials of someone younger, who will stand on their shoulders. This is someone to whom they would like to pass on lessons. The names are called into the circle one by one. At the closing ceremony, the participant reclaims their object as a reminder.

Closing ceremony examples include:

- One-word check-out that describes how participants are feeling.
- Rose, Bud, and Thorn: Each participant is invited to share a Rose (What felt good? What worked well?), a Bud (What are you looking forward to?), and a Thorn (What can be improved?). For groups that do not and will not be meeting often, Rose and Bud can be used alone.
- Laugh Circle: The object of this closing is for circle participants to laugh as a collective. The

laugh increases in tone and then decreases to silence. Encourage participants to move around the room, shake, jump, even roll on the floor. Acknowledge that this may feel silly. This is a great activity to close circles that are high in emotion.

As you can see, being in circle is no small matter. Taking the time to set up and participate mindfully will lead to profound opportunities for transformation and healing. This chapter just scratches the surface of ways in which circles can shift our thinking and our approach to racial healing. We encourage you to learn more about circles and to trust the wisdom of this process, which may feel counterintuitive to many. As Kay Pranis notes in *The Little Book of Circle Processes*, "We are limited only by our imaginations, our willingness to be in respectful and loving relationship with every part of creation, and our ability to allow the pattern of the Circle to emerge without trying to manage or control it."[8]

7.
Working Toward Healing

"These natural laws [of mindfulness], core to the nature of our existence, can offer insight into how we relate to racial distress—specifically, what supports more distress and what supports release from distress."[1]

—Ruth King

As noted in the introduction, we offer a recipe for racial healing, and each chapter so far has offered ingredients. The natural laws of mindfulness that Ruth King refers to above infuse this recipe with yet another ingredient. Restorative justice, trauma awareness and resilience, history, connecting, circles, action, and the elements of this chapter all combine to work toward racial healing, with the intention of transforming damaged or broken pieces of ourselves into wholeness (to the degree possible). We're talking about making an entirely new meal to bring to the table of brother and sisterhood for what Dr.

Martin Luther King Jr. envisioned as our Beloved Community. As a chef would do, you will decide the level of value you derive from these various ingredients—these healing approaches—perhaps altering the amounts or replacing one or more with something different that works for you or your community.

We believe one of the most important questions to ask is, "What would racial healing look like?" It will look different to different people, of course, depending on many factors: who people are, where they come from, what they've experienced, and their connection to the wounds that need healing. The vision for healing also changes and grows as we listen to each other's stories and better understand the wounds.

What Healing Looks Like

Strategies for Trauma Awareness and Resilience (STAR) teaches that a healing journey begins with breaking free from the cycles of violence and moving toward healing through three stages (see Figure 3). The first stage includes finding safety and support. The second stage involves acknowledging what happened to create the wound and responding to the harm with mourning, confronting fear and accepting loss, and committing to take risks.

The final stage toward healing involves reconnecting with parts of ourselves that we may have buried, and with others we may have avoided, shunned, or "othered." This stage suggests some challenging questions:

- Can we engage perpetrators of harm—be they individuals, whole communities, or society in general—and, in doing so, address structural racism?

Figure 3. **Breaking Cycles of Violence • Building Resilience**

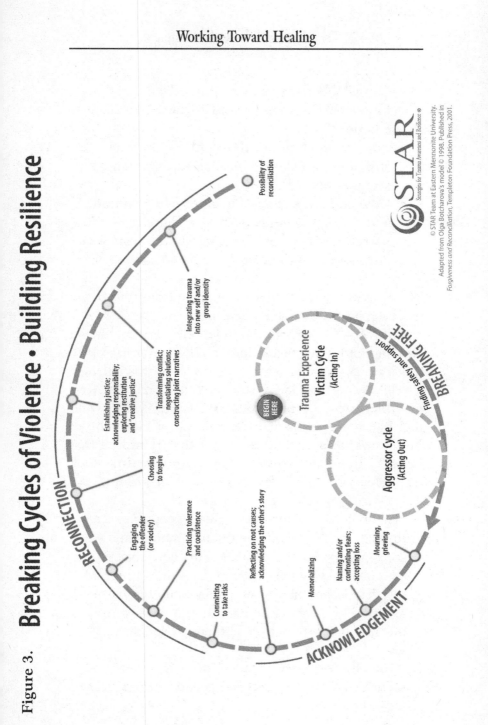

© STAR Team at Eastern Mennonite University.
Adapted from Olga Botcharova's model © 1998. Published in
Forgiveness and Reconciliation, Templeton Foundation Press, 2001.

67

- Can we choose to forgive, understanding that forgiveness is complex and engages our deepest emotions?
- Can we let go of our desire for revenge and still hold perpetrators of racial woundedness accountable?
- How can our various stories of being wounded and causing wounds become a shared narrative? How can we integrate the results of our wounds into our new, evolved selves?

This is the difficult and essential journey we travel on the road toward racial healing.

The W. K. Kellogg Foundation's Truth, Racial Healing and Transformation (TRHT) enterprise provides an example of what is possible on this journey. TRHT teams pondered several questions, the first of which was, "What would the country look and feel like if we jettisoned the belief in a hierarchy of human value and the narratives that reinforce that belief?" In other words, what would healing look like? Here are a few excerpts from their vision:

"We imagine an America where all people are seen through the lens of our common humanity and we see ourselves in one another. This new society is characterized by love, interconnectedness, mutual respect, accountability, empathy, honoring nature and care for the environment. In this society, healing and justice flow from authentic relationships."

"Our children and grandchildren feel safe and secure in who they are and proud of their heritage and culture."

"Memorials serve as a reminder of suffering but also the effort and strength that emerged from it. We no longer carry the pain, fear and shame of history, for we have discovered how to look at our past with courage and honesty."[2]

With this chapter's focus on healing, we invite you to consider what is shared here as you read the following story. Then pause for a few minutes and ask yourself, "What else would healing look like?"

Olga
by Sri Lalitambika Devi

My friend, Olga, has had cancer for two years. I live with her in the women's shelter where I am a residential caretaker. What can I do? I steam mango with sesame seeds, because she thinks this will fight the cancer. I cook whatever else she asks for. She is more a caretaker to me than I am to her, looking in on me each night to smile and say "Good night."

Olga has always liked the name of our shelter. Saranam. The rolling syllables sound mysterious; they are from India. Recently, I thought to translate the name into English for a more universal message. *Saranam* would be better understood as *Refuge*.

This name, she takes issue with. "Refuge. It sounds like a place for slaves to hole up, a stop on the Underground Railroad," she says. She is African American and sensitive to history. "You cannot call this place Refuge," she tells me. And so, we stay as Saranam.

I think about how most of shelter guests are African American and wonder if the cycle of poverty is the new incarnation of slavery that keeps people from living in freedom. I ask Olga, "Why do you think that even after emancipation, so many still struggle for socioeconomic equality?" "Freedom is yet to come," she responds. "We must strive onward."

One evening, I speak of Harriet Tubman as a spiritual leader like Mohammed or Gandhi. In India, we would call her a *mahatma*, a great soul. She is one who achieved hard-won freedom but continued to fight for the liberation of her brothers and sisters, risking her life to guide those still enslaved to the Promised Land. "She is my hero," I say. "You are mine," Olga says. "You don't have to do this, to care about the homeless, but still you offer refuge along the way to our liberation."

Over time, Olga's condition deteriorates, and the powers that be decide she will be transferred to a medical shelter. She does not want to go, but she tells me not to worry; we will both be all right. I miss her, but I carry on. I take refuge in simple tasks like chopping vegetables or folding laundry. This is what Olga hopes for in the end. Clean sheets and no pain. I know that one day she will follow the Drinkin' Gourd, and when I look up into the night sky, she will be there among the infinite points of light.

Multiple Interconnected Paths to Healing

What does healing look like? Just as with recipes, there are a variety of resources and modalities to help address woundedness of body, mind, and spirit. What follows are some that can be used by individuals, groups, and communities. Adapting multiple techniques—these and others—can help personalize and localize the healing journey.

Prayer and Faith. The foundation of most spiritual paths includes concepts of prayer, love, community, faith in a higher power, being in the right relationship (with each other, God, a higher power, the Universe), justice, equality, peace, accountability, kindness, and so on; all the basic tenets of being whole and healed. Participating in a faith community, traveling a spiritual path, engaging in prayer, or maintaining a prayerful approach to life can all contribute to racial healing.

Ceremony and Ritual. Observing and commemorating traumatic events have been part of human life for as long as we have walked the Earth. Ceremony and ritual unify us and connect us with the sacred, with mystery and wonder. Ritual is often considered more formal, a rite that is practiced the same way time after time. Ceremony is often considered less formal, more spontaneous and creative. Ceremonies and rituals can be used to preserve existing traditions and beliefs as well as launching new ones. They can be an honest expression of ethical, moral, and spiritual principles and value and help us connect with our spiritual and sacred beliefs and with whatever we consider to be Divine. They can be cleansing experiences that contribute to racial healing.

71

Mindfulness Meditation. The ability to be mindful in the face of stress and trauma can improve our ability to respond to ourselves and others with kindness, compassion, and wisdom. Ruth King writes, "Being mindful of race is not just about sitting meditation. Mindfulness practice is about changing hearts, and ultimately, having a mindful life."[3] In Bessel van der Kolk's *The Body Keeps the Score*, we learn the critical importance of self-awareness and being in touch with our inner selves, noticing when we become annoyed, nervous, or anxious so we can shift our perspective from our automatic, habitual reactions. Studies have also shown that loving-kindness meditation increases feelings of social connection and can improve automatically activated, implicit attitudes toward stigmatized social groups ("the other").[4]

Memorials, Monuments, and Museums. Statues, memorials, and objects displayed in museums reflect choices, values, and priorities about which historical figures or occurrences are worthy of being remembered. Many that are located in public spaces have become quite controversial. Some have been removed. These memorials influence those who view them. For example, what might someone who views a statue of Martin Luther King Jr. be thinking, versus someone who views a statue of Stonewall Jackson? How might black or white people view such statues differently? Within what context, and with what signage, are various statues located and perceived?

One way to work toward racial healing is to memorialize and contextualize that which caused traumatic racial wounds, as well as the people and events that have contributed to justice, peace, and transformation.

Two new museums have made significant additions to the national conversation about race. The National Museum of African American History and Culture is located on the National Mall in Washington, DC, in view of the White House and the Washington Monument; its location signifies the importance and power of place. The National Memorial for Peace and Justice, created by the Equal Justice Initiative in Montgomery, Alabama, "is the nation's first memorial dedicated to the legacy of enslaved black people, people terrorized by lynching, African Americans humiliated by racial segregation and Jim Crow, and people of color burdened with contemporary presumptions of guilt and police violence."[5]

Apology and Forgiveness. Some of the most profound, and often feared, interactions among people include offering or accepting an apology and forgiving others and ourselves. The benefits of these actions go right to the core of racial healing.

Many white people say or think, "I never enslaved anyone. I wasn't even alive during slavery or even Jim Crow days. Why should I apologize?" Aaron Lazare, in *On Apology*, offers a response when he writes ". . . just as people take pride in things for which they had no responsibility (such as famous ancestors, national championships of their sports teams, and great accomplishments of their nation), so, too, must these people accept the shame (but not guilt) of their family, their athletic teams, and their nations. Accepting national pride must include willingness to accept national shame when one's country has not measured up to reasonable standards." He continues that "people have profited from these actions. Imperialistic acquisition of land and the use of slave labor by a nation, for example, may continue to benefit future generations of citizens. Such beneficiaries, while not guilty, may feel a moral responsibility to those who suffered as a result of the offense."[6] When a person or institution apologizes sincerely and adequately, it is an acknowledgment and expression of remorse for the harm(s) committed. This apology should include a commitment to change and plans for acts of repair/reparation to help restore dignity. It should also demonstrate that the person or institution is committed to shared values and increased safety in the future. In short, the apology must do more than admit past wrongdoing; it must demonstrate that the apologizer is willing and prepared to make amends and to continually make a best effort to do better.

Forgiveness, like apology, is hard work. Within this racial healing approach, such work, often a difficult process, is intended to be done in community. Apology and forgiveness are voluntary acts that cannot be forced. When someone offers forgiveness, they give up many of the emotions, thoughts, and actions seen in the cycles of violence (revenge, dehumanization of "the other," and the good vs. evil narrative). Their healing is no longer tied to other people changing their behaviors and attitudes. There may be varying degrees of forgiveness, related to the profound, centuries-long harm of slavery and racism; the adequacy and quality of the apology; and the particular people involved. It is critical to acknowledge historic and present-day power imbalances and work to overcome them. Successful forgiveness shifts our relationship to power and helps break down walls between two sides. Breaking down systems of power allows us to connect in ways we otherwise cannot. This work is also about being tender with oneself as a way to deconstruct internalized racial oppression. Self-forgiveness is critically important in breaking down barriers and important in overcoming the often-debilitating feelings of shame and guilt. Lazare devotes Chapter 11 of his book to the inextricable tie between apology and forgiveness.

Mourning and Rebirth. When hurt or injury is experienced, it is important to acknowledge the pain and create space to grieve. Grief is often tied to death, and in the case of racial harm, death symbolizes the letting go of shame, guilt, and what holds one back from moving toward racial healing. In many cultures, death is acknowledged through ritual and ceremony. Parkes, Laungani, and Young assert that "death rituals often define the death, the cause of death, the dead person [or thing/feeling you're letting go of], the bereaved, the relationship of the bereaved with one another and with others, and the meaning of life. Failing to carry out necessary rituals or having [them] shortened or undermined can leave people at sea about how the death occurred, who or what the deceased is, how to relate to others, how to think of self, and much more."[7]

There is also dedicated time to mourn. In the Jewish tradition, *shiva* represents the seven days of mourning. "On returning from the funeral, the mourner(s) should be offered a meal prepared by others [. . .] and during the whole *shiva* period they may not work, nor should they prepare their own food; their needs must be tended as far as possible by others."[8] This part of the ritual had a high emphasis on care and community support to provide time and space for mourning.

The National Memorial for Peace and Justice, which honors more than four thousand African American people lynched by white mobs in the nineteenth and twentieth centuries, encourages the collecting of dirt from sites of lynchings across America, remembering and saying aloud the names of victims, and inscribing their names on permanent monuments. These are living rituals representing death and mourning, and also rebirth. Whatever release happens through mourning lays the ground for something new to be born in that soil. Specifically, the Peace and Justice Memorial is a way to cleanse that space and name it as sacred, something other than simply a site of lynching.

There are many more healing resources available, and the book *The Body Keeps the Score* explores a wide range of possibilities. Many have used therapy, neurofeedback, PTSD treatment, yoga, breathwork, and the Hawaiian process of Ho'oponopono. Others turn to the arts and find healing in music, theater (including playback theater), painting, writing, and dance (including InterPlay and Dance Exchange). Whatever feels like it might help, try it. Trust your heart. Work with friends in a supportive community. Teach your children. Be that change in the world you wish to see. Together, we can work toward racial healing by any and all means available.

8.
Taking Action

*"There are risks and costs to a program of action.
But they are far less than the long-range risks and
costs of comfortable inaction."*
—John F. Kennedy

We're sure you can feel that trauma awareness,
restorative justice, circles, and each of the
three pillars presented thus far—uncovering history,
making connections, and working toward healing—
all involve risks and costs. Each pillar also involves
and supports taking action, the fourth pillar. Sitting
in circle with other people committed to racial healing and exploring touchstones and values is a form of
taking action. Becoming knowledgeable about trauma
and its impact and learning to be resilient in the face
of trauma is a form of taking action. Learning about
how justice can be achieved in ways that are restorative and transformative, rather than simply punitive,
is a form of taking action. All require action on your
part to move forward in this racial healing journey.
We hope this book inspires you to act to repair the

racial harm, to the degree possible. We offer some final action ideas for you to consider.

Continue to Educate Yourself

Read more to continue building your knowledge about racial injustice and healing, deepening your self-awareness of your own stories, and gathering ideas for taking action. There are many relevant and useful resources available now; we offer recommendations at the end of this book. Watch films, go to plays, and sign up for classes, trainings, webinars, and workshops offered by colleges and universities, non-profits, and community groups. We also recommend damali ayo's 2007 guide, "I Can Fix It." She asked 2,000 people what individuals can do to end racism and compiled the results into two lists of five action steps—one list for white people and the other for people of color. Here are a few excerpts:[1]

For white people:

1. Admit you have a race and that racism exists.
2. Listen to people of color. Honor their experience and outrage.
3. Educate yourself. Seriously.
4. Broaden your experience (but please don't do this before completing steps 1–3). Learn about other cultures and put yourself into environments predominantly attended by people of color.
5. Take action and consider racism your problem to solve.

For people of color:

1. Be yourself. Don't play into white, negative stereotypes. Love yourself and one another.
2. Speak out. Talk and listen to white people. Make your presence known.
3. Educate yourself about the accomplishments of people of color. Teach your kids to have pride in who they are. Deal with your own issues of prejudice.
4. Build ties. Resist segregation. Cultivate relationships with white people you like.
5. Take care. You don't have to educate white people. Make your health and sanity a priority.

Engage Your Community

Racial healing is not solo work; it is collective work, done in community. So, how best to engage people in your community? The Kellogg Foundation's Truth, Racial Healing and Transformation enterprise (TRHT, introduced in Chapter 7) offers examples, recommendations, and inspirational ideas for actions you can take in your own community through the *TRHT Implementation Guidebook*. The ideas offered in the guidebook are organized around five foundational pillars: narrative change, racial healing, separation, law, and economics. The narrative change recommendations seek to create a more complete and accurate narrative to help people understand how systems of racial hierarchy have been, and continue to be, embedded in our society in areas such as entertainment, journalism, digital and social media, school curricula, museums, cultural institutions, and literature. These systems affect the way we communicate and can influence people's perspectives, perceptions, and behaviors about and toward one another. Understanding the systems will help us work more effectively and productively together toward community-based change. The racial healing recommendations focus on how we can heal from historic wounds and build mutually respectful relationships across racial and ethnic lines.

Three other foundational pillars focus on action items related to core societal institutions in which the belief in a hierarchy of human value is embedded and evidenced:

1. **Separation:** Explore the mix of laws, policies, structures, habits, and biases that create and sustain separation (physical, social, and psychological) according to racial categories and result in the subjugation of particular cultures, values, and languages. Then address the impacts of separation, which has led to concentrated poverty in neighborhoods, with the goal of ensuring equitable access to health, education, and jobs.

2. **Law:** Review discriminatory civil and criminal laws and public policies and explore and recommend solutions that will lead to systems that reflect our common humanity and the dignity of everyone and systems with just applications of laws and policies that reflect a commitment to the civil and human rights of all, including redress of past inequities.

3. **Economy:** Study structured inequality
   and barriers to economic opportunities and
   recommend transformative approaches to create
   an equitable society for all people regardless
   of racial, ethnic, or cultural background.

The TRHT enterprise relies on dialogue and acknowledges that "after participants get to know one another and build relationships, the process also involves developing a plan for creating transformational change in one or more areas [listed above]—the things that keep us apart like residential segregation and colonization."[2]

Engage in Truth-Telling

In the summer of 2014, Michael Brown Jr., an eighteen-year-old African American man, was shot and killed by a twenty-eight-year-old white police officer. His body laid lifeless for over three hours before being removed by the county medical examiner's office. Before his name was called through the streets along with the chant "Hands up! Don't shoot!" many couldn't locate Ferguson on a map. Today, we all know the name of Michael Brown Jr. and the city in which his murder occurred. The young people of Ferguson led the charge of telling the truth of what happened as the nation watched, and others from across the country went to Ferguson, just as they went to Mississippi in 1964 during Freedom Summer. The story of Michael Brown Jr. and Ferguson exemplifies how we must first tell the truth in order for the possibilities of healing to unfold.

Ferguson continues to tell the truth. Out of this tragedy rose the Truth Telling Project,[3] which seeks

81

to create opportunities for storytelling as a process to disrupt police violence and institutional racism. One way that this takes place is through public meetings where community members share experiences. In November 2015, the Truth Telling Project hosted a national event entitled "A Night of a Thousand Conversations." The truth-telling live stream of individuals sharing experiences of police terrorism and harm was viewed all across the county. Viewers were encouraged to have their own conversations afterward, using a project toolkit. This was a bottom-up approach that started from the roots, with the people.

The outcome of such truth-telling efforts is unpredictable. They may or may not result in apologies, forgiveness, or reconciliation. These may be hoped-for goals for many participants, but as David Ragland, Cori Bush, and Melinda Salazar, members of the Truth Telling Project Steering Committee, suggest, "Reconciliation and forgiveness is not always possible in the wake of ongoing trauma. Many transitional justice, healing, and trauma specialists understand the detrimental effects of forcing people to forgive their assailants."[4]

The process of truth-telling in a safe space is the first step toward breaking free. It's important to note that the burden of forgiveness and reconciliation is not the primary responsibility of the oppressed and marginalized.

We noted the challenges regarding apology and forgiveness in the previous chapter. The concept of reconciliation between European Americans and African Americans in the United States is also deeply fraught. We are not suggesting there was once a healthy relationship prior to colonization that we recommend reconciling, restoring, or returning to. Rather, we refer to the broader vision of restoring our humanity; becoming our best selves, individually and collectively.

Truth-telling can be practiced through talking to your neighbors. Getting proximate helps to form new ideas and beliefs based on experiences rather than assumptions. Join a local community social justice organization, attend events, and seek to create intentional spaces for conversations. The circle process and White Ally Toolkit (discussed later in this chapter) are resources to encourage your next steps.

There is a rising call for truth-telling as it relates to racial violence and inequity on a national level, which has resulted in an exploration of establishing a Truth Commission in the United States to examine violence against African Americans. Precedence for such exists with smaller processes in Greensboro, North Carolina, in response to the 1979 massacre, and the Samuel Dewitt Proctor Conference Truth-telling Commission on racial and economic justice in Memphis, Tennessee. Restorative justice warrior and healer Fania Davis has called for a process that centers on restorative justice. In a 2016 *Yes!* magazine interview with Fania and Angela Davis, Fania makes the claim, "A lot of people think that restorative justice can only address interpersonal harm—and it's very successful in that. But the truth and reconciliation model is one that's supposed to address mass harm—to heal the wounds of structural violence. [. . .] In addition to that sort of hearing commission structure, there could be circles happening on the local levels—circles between, say, persons who were victims of violence and the persons who caused them

83

harm." Angela challenges us by asking, "How does one imagine accountability for someone representing the state who has committed unspeakable acts of violence?"[5] This is the challenge we face as a nation. It is easy to be punitive and make others disposable. The difficult task is in telling the truth in ways that seek healing and transformation.

What truth-telling needs to be done in your community? What historical harms and present-day systems and structures need addressing? No doubt there are historical articles or books that have been written about your community. You and your colleagues will find it useful to ensure such historical records include connections to racism and the legacies and aftermath of slavery and other stories of oppression and injustice.

Support Reparations

Randall Robinson calls for reparations when he writes, "At long last, let America contemplate the scope of its enduring human-rights wrong against the whole of a people. Let the vision of blacks not become so blighted from a sunless eternity that we fail to *see* the staggering breadth of America's crime against us."[6]

Let's face it: The word "reparations" freaks out a lot of white people. The reaction typically goes something like this: "Why should I pay for something I didn't do? I never enslaved anyone," or "Why should black people today receive reparations? They were never enslaved." But an honest look at American history reveals that the system of enslavement caused great harm to people of African descent and provided great benefit and privilege to people of European descent. The *living* consequences of that system continue to affect every person in the United States today.

Whether white people feel personal responsibility for the legacy of slavery or not is irrelevant. We all have a moral and ethical obligation to support each other, create the best world we can, and repair or transform systems that benefit some people over others based on race (or gender, religion, class, or any other factor). Anything we don't repair or transform, we will pass on to our children and grandchildren, perpetuating injustice and inequality through inaction.

The Chicago Torture Justice Center serves as an example of reparation. Chicago Police Department Commander Jon Burge, and police officers under his command, tortured over 120 African Americans into giving false confessions between 1972 and 1991. In 2015, the Chicago City Council passed a Reparations Ordinance (the first municipality in the United States to do so), which established the Chicago Torture Justice Center. In supporting the movement to end police violence, the center provides specialized trauma services to those tortured by law enforcement officers, as well as their family members, including their grandchildren. Other reparation features of the ordinance include a formal apology from the mayor and city council, a permanent public memorial, inclusion in the Chicago public school curriculum, as well as free tuition or job training, job placement, access to support services, and the creation of a reparations fund of $5.5 million for torture survivors.[7]

Coming to the Table (CTTT) has also explored the meaning of, and possibilities for, reparations. A working group committed to the topic solicited and received input over three years to develop the reparations guide, "Reparations: The Time is Now!"[8] This free downloadable guide includes short-term

85

and long-term action items, organized around the four CTTT pillars, for individuals, communities, and society. The guide seeks to inspire European Americans to action while taking their cues from African Americans as to when and how to approach and implement reparations. African Americans may also wish to engage in some of the activities to ensure that trust, healing, and true reparation of harm are achieved. The guide also challenges this nation's relationship with capitalism and money. Repair does not simply come through funding the college education of a descendant or giving to an organization of color. Repair requires getting proximate in order to face the hard truths and acknowledge the social and destructive construction of race. Reparation is about a transformation, not a transaction.

Become a White Ally and Accomplice

If you are a white person reading this book, you have probably heard the terms "white ally" and "white accomplice." There has been debate over the terms. For some, the concept of being a social justice "ally" has become synonymous with feeling good but being ineffective. An accomplice, however, works together with marginalized individuals and groups to dismantle the structures and systems causing the marginalization and injustice. Without minimizing the importance of debate over this language, we stress the critical importance of white people working for justice from their positions of privilege.

One powerful tool we recommend is the White Ally Toolkit developed by Dr. David Campt. This popular toolkit and program focuses on active listening, empathy, and storytelling to promote racial equity. The approach is based on "dialogic learning, which is essentially about the process of people learning about a social reality by (1) starting with their own experiences, (2) moving to other people's experiences, [and] (3) raising questions about why people's experiences are similar and different."[9] You may also want to consider joining Showing Up for Racial Justice (SURJ), a national network of individuals and groups working for racial justice and an end to white supremacy. SURJ has chapters across the country. Check their website for a group near you.[10]

The importance of white people working with, and talking to, other white people about whiteness, privilege, power, othering, and racism cannot be overstated. The power in racism rests with whiteness. Dismantling systems of white supremacy, injustice, inequity, and oppression is the responsibility of white people.

Nat Turner Killed My Family
by Sheri Bailey

I was working on Juneteenth* business when my colleague's wife came into the office and said a woman outside needed to talk to me. Confused, I went outside where a young Black woman explained how she saw a pickup truck hit my car and speed off. I had been assaulted by a thoughtless stranger, but what started off as buzzard's luck turned into something profound. After locating my assailant,

* Juneteenth celebrates the signing of the Emancipation Proclamation and the end of slavery in the United States. Sheri Bailey is the founder of JuneteenthVA in Virginia.

the detective casually mentioned that the man's pickup sported a Confederate flag emblem on its back bumper! Up until then, whenever I saw the rebel flag, I went nuclear. But with this incident of an ignorant young man hitting my car, I came to realize it is not about me telling folks they shouldn't embrace their symbols. Nowadays, I only have a problem when a state flies that symbol over its capital.

My play *Abolitionists' Museum* features eight historical characters: John Brown, Frederick Douglass, Abraham Lincoln, Harriet Beecher Stowe, Sojourner Truth, Harriet Tubman, Nat Turner, and David Walker. In the play, they are wax figures in a museum, where the curator has recently placed a Confederate flag, who debate and subsequently vote about whether or not to burn the controversial cloth. During one performance, a woman interrupted and directed these words at the actor playing Nat Turner: "My name is Rose Nichols, and Nat Turner killed my family!" She said it like it happened recently and not 178 years previously!

As a playwright, I'm tasked with telling these stories. And as a Black woman of color whose ancestor gave birth to the universe in which we all now live, I am compelled from the depths of my DNA to help others give witness to how, through daily acts of simple decency and courage, we can lift up those who would be burdens. An eyewitness reporting a minor traffic incident and a detective doing his job make our communities stronger. An elderly woman coming to see a play being presented by people whom she assumes will not understand her pain gives me hope.

Taking action to address historical harms is a long and continuous process and can take cn many forms. It is hard work, and it is good work. It requires engaging all relevant stakeholders, building trust, humanizing each other (especially those we consider "the other"), and identifying and overcoming barriers to working together toward solutions. Do an assessment of what various organizations are already doing in your community. Find ways to collaborate, which can lighten the burden. Substantial action will require organization, leadership, and resources. Most important, and perhaps most obvious, find what you can do, and do it.

9.
Liberation and Transformation

Kimberly James, author of *Finding My Brave Space: A Black Girl's Tale of Wanderlust*, participated in a three-day workshop we co-facilitated in 2017, in which we shared the approach outlined in these pages. Several months after the workshop, she flew to Ghana. On her Facebook page, she wrote how she loved being among all the black folks on the plane from London to Accra. She was inspired to write the following. She called it rough and unpolished. We found it inspiring and perfect for this closing chapter.

the Point. the Center. the Norm.

It feels good to be here
On this plane filled with black people of all
*   shades, hair textures and styles.*
People speaking different languages.
Filling economy, business, first class.
Friends
Families and couples

Kids
laughing, working, reading, sleeping. Being.
the Point. the Center. the Norm.

My heart swells with joy because it is not often
    that I am
the Point. the Center. the Norm.
If you're white in America, in much of the world,
    really, you're used to being
the Point. the Center. the Norm.

What was it like to grow up being
the Point. the Center. the Norm?
To not be the only one on your street or in your
    class?
To not have teachers equate your skin tone with
    the lack of intelligence?
To not feel the sizzle of a hot comb or the burn of
    chemicals so your hair could meet a standard of
    beauty?
To not have rules that won't allow you to wear
    your hair the way it naturally grows out of your
    head?
To have the powers that be say banning locs and
    braids is not against the law because they go
    against
the Point. the Center. the Norm.
To not be regarded as dangerous, criminal, angry?

But don't we have the right to be Angry?
Look how quickly you get angry when you're asked
    to make space for others in
the Point. the Center. the Norm.

Cries of:
All lives matter.
Reverse racism.
Make.
America.
Great.
Again.
When was it great for me?
When black people were held in bondage and sold
  like property?
When Jim Crow ruled the land, terrorized families
  and strange fruit hung from a tree?
When separate was anything but equal and we
  needed a Green Book to travel safely?
When Police brutalize Black bodies at will and
  then get acquitted?
When standing up for your rights gets you hosed,
  fired, assassinated?
When we're told that it's not the right time to
  speak out against injustice. It's not the right way
  or the right time?
the Point. the Center. the Norm.

If you're black in America, and much of the world,
  really. It's an unfamiliar place.
You're used to being located outside of
the Point. the Center. the Norm.
Your skin tone and hair judged by a standard that
  doesn't fit you.
The way you speak and move through the world
  degraded, mocked, villainized because it does
  not originate from
the Point. the Center. the Norm.
How was it decided?

the Point. the Center. the Norm.
Who said one way was THE way?
the Point. the Center. the Norm.

I see now
the threat of having
the Point. the Center. the Norm
challenged.

It's a powerful position to be in.
It's comfortable
It's safe
It's privileged

I like being
the Point. the Center. the Norm.
Many people ask me, why Africa?
I could talk about the variety of cultures, nature or
    the historic sites, but I have a simple answer.
For a little while I get to breathe free and be
the Point.
the Center.
the Norm.

Kimberly's observations are what we hope this little book inspires all of us to build toward through our healing work. She and Tom first met in 2001 on the Rhode Island set for the filming of the documentary *Traces of the Trade: A Story from the Deep North*. He was one of the family members featured in the film. She was one of a group of people who volunteered to participate one weekend in conversations about the issues that emerged during the journey the family took to retrace the triangle slave trade route of their ancestors.

93

At one point in the film, Juanita Browne, one of the producers and also a woman of color, sat in circle, in a hotel room in Ghana, with the family of ten white descendants of slave traders as they attempted to navigate their way toward a better understanding of contemporary race relations. When asked for her impressions of what the family was doing, she expressed her anger at white people for their cowardice and their choice to give up their integrity and humanity for so long:

> *Knowing what has happened to my people; it's ridiculous! If you grew up where I grew up, you'd be pissed off! Anybody who is alive, or who is paying attention, should be pissed off. The fact that white people are not pissed off means they're not paying attention.*
>
> *And it's helpful for me. The reason why I'm doing this is because it's important for me that white people take responsibility. Ultimately, it's about human liberation. And also, it's about liberation of my people. It's about liberation of you guys. That's the truth.*[1]

Two women of color. Two journeys to Ghana, sixteen years apart. Strikingly similar messages.

A Message from Tom

I sat in that circle in Ghana, in July 2001, with Juanita and my cousins. I have watched this exchange between Juanita and Elly (and the rest of us) at screenings of the film probably one hundred times over the years. It is one of the key messages from the film and one of the key messages I hope people take

94

away from this book: *It is important that white people take responsibility* because *it is about liberation.* It is about the liberation of all of us.

As a white man, I am grateful to have learned of my connection to racism, the legacy and aftermath of slavery, white supremacy, and the present-day impacts of all of it. And no, this connection has very little to do with being related to slave traders. It has to do with "whiteness" itself and the fact that, long ago, people who saw themselves as white and superior (the Point. the Center. the Norm.) created this thing we know as racism to benefit themselves, their families, and their descendants. They did so at the expense of black people and other people of color, who white people determined were inferior. It is money and power that lead to separation, brokenness, trauma, and fear. Most important, and oddly bewildering, is that it seems that white people know the least about whiteness and its impacts.

I have no interest in making white people feel guilty or ashamed about the past or the present. Guilt just leads to building walls of self-protection and separation. No, my interest is in inspiring white people to understand and embrace what Rev. Dr. King wrote in his "Letter from a Birmingham Jail": "Injustice anywhere is a threat to justice everywhere. We are caught in an inescapable network of mutuality, tied in a single garment of destiny. Whatever affects one directly, affects all indirectly." Understanding that we are all in this journey together—truly and profoundly interconnected—*in an inescapable network of mutuality* is a critical step in racial healing.

Another step, a most crucial step necessary to begin racial healing, is for white people to scrutinize and understand whiteness and to acknowledge and own our role in the perpetuation and dismantling of racism.

If you are white and feeling uncomfortable, that is okay. This work is often uncomfortable. If you find yourself feeling defensive and argumentative, or guilty and ashamed, please stop. Remember Chapter 2? That's your emotional brain kicking in. Engage your rational brain and explore your whiteness. Do your homework. Talk with other white people who also want to learn about this stuff and change. Understand that you are going to make mistakes and say the wrong thing sometimes. Own that, as well. Apologize and change your thoughts, words, and behavior. Speak out against injustice. Teach your children. Be the change.

In these challenging days, when white supremacists are emboldened by the words and example of a US president to create more racial havoc, it is more important than ever for white people to stand up, speak out, and take action for racial justice and healing, dismantle racist systems and structures, and work toward transformation and liberation for everyone. Use the advantages whiteness affords you to make a positive difference.

A Message from Jodie

I do not have any profound words of wisdom for black people and other people of color. I have my experiences and I am on this journey to liberation and transformation with you. When your heart breaks, there's an echo in the hollow of mine. In the past, liberation and the process of freedom, in my mind, had always been interconnected with changing systems. While I asked for justice through policy change and advocated for restorative justice with a racial justice lens, I was also asking to be free. It felt like a destination, rather than a journey of breaking internalized and external chains. I had given up my power in some aspects, so that my liberation became about tearing down walls and bars that cage young people, queer people, black people, and others who did not fit into some box or master narrative. While structures of institutional and economic injustice continue to perpetuate harm, it is not my work alone to rinse the blood of colonization off my back while it runs down my face.

It was not until a conversation with a college mentor that I realized what was possible. Jada and I sat in a hotel room reconnecting and laughing about my undergrad days and journey to Oakland, California. We dreamed together of our desires during this time of deep hope and deep despair across this nation. Without much thought I said, "I'm trying to get free." She responded, "Aren't you free? I feel free." I paused. My temple throbbed. I did not have an answer. I do not ever remember anyone asking me this question before. Her words have stayed with me.

I remember being so angry as a young organizer. With every protest, action, and meeting that feeling grew into despair and was sometimes counterproductive to my well-being. I had internalized the racist beliefs and thoughts white supremacy taught me. The ideas were often about my beauty, intelligence, and right to live in a dignified way. I sometimes thought I wasn't deserving of freedom. I realized that I was trying to convince non-black people that we mattered, and I was more than the color of my skin. I needed to begin defining myself for myself. Blackness is expansive. It doesn't begin and end with slavery. I am much more than the generational harm of white supremacy and colonization.

Liberation and Transformation

"We are wired to be caring for the other and generous to one another. We shrivel when we are not able to interact. I mean that is part of the reason why solitary confinement is such a horrendous punishment. We depend on the other in order for us to be fully who we are. I didn't know that I was going to come so soon to the concept that we have at home, the concept of Ubuntu. It says: A person is a person through other persons."[2]
—Archbishop Desmond Tutu

Transformation and liberation are about remembrance. We begin to reclaim our humanity when we remember our interconnectedness and share with each other. We trust you will find the metaphor of coming to the table and sharing meals together and following and modifying recipes useful. We are all hungry. Once we commit to coming to the table together, we gather the ingredients, follow the recipe, and make the food. The joy is in eating and in sharing the meal. In this case, the table serves as a center, which grounds all that is heavy and all that is light. Let us eat with our hands because it provides an intimate and direct connection with our meal that we cannot get with a knife and fork. Indeed, newborns first receive nourishment through direct connection with their mothers. Then, when they begin to eat solid food, they do so with their hands. Then the world intrudes, and we teach them to use spoons and forks, just as we were taught. But our hands provide direct connection. Feel that taco? That sandwich? Similarly, our hands are the utensils we need to reach out and hold one another—and, realistically, to sometimes let go. There is no shame in getting dirty. There is no judgment for seeking another serving. There is enough for each of us. There is more, for all of us. This is exactly what we need.

Following this chapter is a section of recommended reading; that is, more ingredients in the recipes for circles, restorative justice, trauma awareness, history, connection, healing, and action. Help us create a new meal by continuing your journey of learning, truth-telling, liberation, and transformation.

Racial healing is heart and soul work; *your* heart and soul work. The only person you can truly change is yourself. So know yourself and be committed to learning, without harming. As you work with others, do so mindfully and with care. We need to stay at the table together to transform together. Coming to the table is the easy part. *Staying* at the table is the hard part; make the commitment to stay when things get hard. Racial healing—and, by extension, healing all forms of oppression and injustice—is about transforming our thoughts, beliefs, emotions, and instincts so that our sole/soul focus is on transforming and liberating ourselves, our communities, our systems, and our world.

Let it be so.

Recommended Reading

As noted, this is a Little Book about a very BIG topic. With this brief introduction to this approach to racial healing, we encourage you to continue your research, expand your understanding, and enhance your effectiveness in this important work. We offer the following resources, with chapter-by-chapter relevance, to get you started. Many more recommendations can be found at www.comingto thetable.org/lbrh.

Chapter 2: Trauma Awareness and Resilience

- *The Little Book of Trauma Healing*, and Peace After Trauma website, with resources, webinars and a STAR-basics self-paced course: https: //peaceaftertrauma.com/ (both by Carolyn Yoder)
- *The Body Keeps the Score*, by Bessel van der Kolk
- *The New Jim Crow: Mass Incarceration in the Age of Colorblindness*, by Michelle Alexander
- The fundamentals of epigenetics: https://www .whatisepigenetics.com/fundamentals/

Chapter 3: Restorative Justice

- *The Little Book of Restorative Justice*, by Howard Zehr
- *Restorative Justice in Urban Schools: Disrupting the School-to-Prison Pipeline*, by Anita Wadhwa
- *A Restorative Justice Reader*, edited by Gerry Johnstone
- *Returning to the Teachings: Exploring Aboriginal Justice*, by Rupert Ross

Chapter 4: Uncovering History

- *An Indigenous People's History of the United States*, by Roxanne Dunbar-Ortiz
- *A Brief History of Everyone Who Ever Lived: The Human Story Retold Through Our Genes*, by Adam Rutherford
- *Stamped from the Beginning*, by Ibram X. Kendi
- *The Cross and the Lynching Tree*, by James Cone
- *The Color of Law: A Forgotten History of How Our Government Segregated America*, by Richard Rothstein

Chapter 5: Making Connections

- *The Healing Art of Storytelling*, by Richard Stone
- *Microaggressions in Everyday Life: Race, Gender, and Sexual Orientation*, by Derald Wing Sue
- *The Four Agreements: A Practical Guide to Personal Freedom*, by Don Miguel Ruiz

Chapter 6: Circles, Touchstones, and Values

- *The Little Book of Circle Processes*, by Kay Pranis
- *Calling the Circle: The First and Future Culture*, by Christina Baldwin
- *Wild & Wise: Sacred Feminine Meditations for Women's Circles & Personal Awakening*, by Amy Bammel Wilding
- *Circle Forward: Building a Restorative School Community*, by Carolyn Boyles-Watson and Kay Pranis

Chapter 7: Working Toward Healing

- *Mindful of Race: Transforming Racism from the Inside Out*, by Ruth King
- *Radical Forgiveness*, by Colin Tipping
- *Zero Limits: The Secret Hawaiian System for Wealth, Health, Peace, and More*, by Joe Vitale and Ihaleakala Hew Len
- *My Grandmother's Hands: Racialized Trauma and the Pathway to Mending Our Hearts and Bodies*, by Resmaa Menakem
- *Free Your Mind: An African American Guide to Meditation and Freedom*, by Cortez R. Rainey

Chapter 8: Taking Action

- The White Ally Toolkit: https://www.whiteally toolkit.com/
- *Just Mercy: A Story of Justice and Redemption*, by Bryan Stevenson

- *Uprooting Racism: How White People Can Work for Racial Justice*, by Paul Kivel
- *Why Are All The Black Kids Sitting Together in the Cafeteria?* by Beverly Daniel Tatum
- *The Debt: What America Owes to Blacks* by Randall Robinson

Chapter 9: Liberation and Transformation

- *White Fragility: Why It's So Hard for White People to Talk About Racism*, by Robin DiAngelo
- *Well, That Escalated Quickly: Memoirs and Mistakes of an Accidental Activist*, by Franchesca Ramsey
- *Privilege, Power, and Difference*, by Allan G. Johnson
- *Tears We Cannot Stop: A Sermon to White America*, by Michael Eric Dyson

Notes

Chapter 1: Introduction

1 Thomas Norman DeWolf, *Inheriting the Trade* (Boston: Beacon Press, 2009), 99.
2 DeWolf, *Inheriting the Trade*, 99.

Chapter 2: Trauma Awareness and Resilience

1 Bessel van der Kolk, MD, *The Body Keeps the Score: Brain, Mind, and Body in the Healing of Trauma* (New York: Viking, 2014), 1.
2 "Trauma Overview, Stress and Trauma Definitions," participant manual, STAR Seminar, (Eastern Mennonite University, 2004), 2.
3 Carolyn Yoder, *The Little Book of Trauma Healing* (Intercourse, PA: Good Books, 2005), 6.
4 David Anderson Hooker and Amy Potter Czajkowski, *Transforming Historical Harms* (http://comingtothetable.org/wp-content/uploads/2013/10/01-Transforming_Historical_Harms.pdf), 27.
5 Hooker and Czajkowski, *Transforming Historical Harms,* 28.
6 The Gilder Lehrman Institute of American History: https://www.gilderlehrman.org/content/historical-context-facts-about-slave-trade-and-slavery.

7   Edward E. Baptist, *The Half Has Never Been Told: Slavery and the Making of American Capitalism* (New York: Basic Books, 2014), 41.

8   Toni Morrison, *The Origin of Others* (Cambridge, MA: Harvard University Press, 2017), 28–29.

9   Adam Rutherford, *A Brief History of Everyone Who Ever Lived* (New York: The Experiment, 2017), 81.

Chapter 3: Restorative Justice

1   Claudia Rankine, "The Condition of Black Life Is One of Mourning," in *The Fire This Time*, ed. Jesmyn Ward (New York: Scribner, 2016, 150.

2   Howard Zehr, *The Little Book of Restorative Justice* (Intercourse, PA: Good Books, 2002), 21.

3   Zehr, *Little Book of Restorative Justice*, 21

4   Zehr, *Little Book of Restorative Justice*, 22–24.

5   Michael Harriot, "Why We Never Talk About Black-on-Black Crime: An Answer to White America's Most Pressing Question," *The Root*, October 3, 2017, https://www.theroot.com/why -we-never-talk-about-black-on-black-crime-an -answer-1819092337.

6   "NAACP Criminal Justice Fact Sheet," https://www.naacp.org/criminal-justice-fact-sheet/.

7   Marc Lamont Hill, *Nobody: Casualties of America's War on the Vulnerable, from Ferguson to Flint and Beyond* (New York: Atria Books, 2016), xix–xx.

8   Steven Hsieh, "14 Disturbing Stats about Racial Inequality in American Public Schools," *The Nation*, March 21, 2014, https://www.thenation.com/article /14-disturbing-stats-about-racial-inequality-american -public-schools/.

9   Restorative Justice for Oakland Youth, "About Us," http://rjoyoakland.org/about/.

10 Anita Wadhwa, *Restorative Justice in Urban Schools: Disrupting the School-to-Prison Pipeline* (New York: Routledge, 2015), 18.

11 Donna Hicks, *Dignity: Its Essential Role in Resolving Conflict* (New Haven, CT: Yale University Press, 2011), 4.

Chapter 4: Uncovering History

1 Howard Zinn, *A People's History of the United States* (New York: Harper Collins, 2003), 23.

2 bell hooks, *Teaching to Transgress: Education as the Practice of Freedom* (New York: Routledge, 1994), 24.

3 Malcolm Gladwell, "Miss Buchanan's Period of Adjustment," *Revisionist History* podcast, Episode 3, Season 2, June 28, 2018. Podcast: http://revisionist history.com/episodes/13-miss-buchanans-period -of-adjustment. Transcript: https://blog.simonsays .ai/miss-buchanans-period-of-adjustment-revisionist -history-podcast-transcript-b4c65731f73c.

4 Ira Katznelson, *When Affirmative Action Was White: An Untold History of Racial Inequality in Twentieth-Century America* (New York: W.W. Norton & Company, 2005), 113–141.

5 Equal Justice Initiative, "Lynching in America: Confronting the Legacy of Racial Terror," https://eji .org/reports/lynching-in-america.

6 Ibram X. Kendi, *Stamped from the Beginning: The Definitive History of Racist Ideas in America* (New York: Nation Books, 2016), 4.

Chapter 5: Making Connections

1 Richard Stone, *The Healing Art of Storytelling: A Sacred Journey of Personal Discovery* (New York: Authors Choice Press, 2004), 3.

2   Project Implicit: https://implicit.harvard.edu/implicit /education.html.
3   Stone, *Healing Art of Storytelling*, 3.
4   Coming to the Table provides a guide on starting a group in your community among the resources on its website. Though focused on CTTT affiliates, the principles apply to any group of people committed to working together on challenging issues and transformation: http://comingtothetable.org /wp-content/uploads/2018/09/Starting-a-CTTT -Local-Affiliate-Group.pdf.

Chapter 6: Circle Process, Touchstones, and Values

1   Alice Walker, *The Cushion in the Road* (New York: New Press, 2013), 286.
2   Kay Pranis, *The Little Book of Circle Processes: A New/Old Approach to Peacemaking* (Intercourse, PA: Good Books, 2005), 3.
3   Kay Pranis, Barry Stuart, and Mark Wedge, *Peacemaking Circles: From Crime to Community* (St. Paul, MN: Living Justice Press, 2003), 70–71.
4   Rutherford, *Brief History*, 218.
5   "Why Does Privilege Make People So Angry?" *Decoded*, MTV News, video, https://www.youtube .com/watch?v = qeYpvV3eRhY.
6   For more on understanding "the problem as the problem and not people as the problem," see David Anderson Hooker, *The Little Book of Transformative Community Conferencing* (New York: Good Books, 2016), 50.
7   Toucshtones adapted from: Ann Holmes Redding and Pat Russell, "Touchstones," Coming to the Table, accessed October 15, 2018, http://comingtothetable

.org/wp-content/uploads/2018/10/TOUCHSTONES
.pdf.

8   Pranis, *Little Book of Circle Processes*, 69.

Chapter 7: Working Toward Healing

1   Ruth King, *Mindful of Race: Transforming Racism From the Inside Out* (Boulder, CO: Sounds True, 2018), 4.

2   W. K. Kellogg Foundation, "TRHT Design Team Recommendations," December 2016, 19, http://coming tothetable.org/wp-content/uploads/2016/01 /TRHT-Design-Team-Recs.pdf.

3   King, *Mindful of Race*, 128.

4   Loving-kindness meditations: Cendri A. Hutcherson, Emma M. Seppala, and James J. Gross, "Loving-kindness meditation increases social connectedness," *Emotion* 8, no. 5 (2008): 720–724, doi: 10.1037/ a0013237. Yoona Kang, Jeremy R. Gray, and John F. Dovidio, "The non-discriminating heart: Loving-kindness meditation training decreases implicit intergroup bias," *Journal of Experimental Psychology* 143, no. 3 (2014): 1306–1313, doi: 10.1037/a0034150. Alexander J. Stell and Tom Farsides, "Brief loving-kindness meditation reduces racial bias mediated by positive other-regarding emotions," *Motivation and Emotion* 40, no. 1 (2016): 140–147, doi: 10.1007/s11031-015-9514-x.

5   Equal Justice Initiative, "The National Memorial for Peace and Justice," https://eji.org/national-lynching -memorial.

6   Aaron Lazare, *On Apology* (New York: Oxford University Press, 2004), 41–42.

7   Colin Murray Parkes, Pittu Laungani, and William Young, eds., *Death and Bereavement Across Cultures*: Second edition (New York: Routledge, 2015), 27.

8   Norman Solomon, *Historical Dictionary of Judaism*: Third Edition (Lanham, MD: Rowman & Littlefield, 2015), 125.

Chapter 8: Taking Action

1   Provided with permission from damali ayo "I Can Fix It," accessed October 15, 2018, http://comingto thetable.org/wp-content/uploads/2018/08/ICF_FREE .pdf.
2   "TRHT Implementation Guidebook," http://www .racialequityresourceguide.org/TRHTSummit.
3   The Truth Telling Project: http://www.thetruth tellingproject.org/.
4   David Ragland, Cori Bush, and Melinda Salazar, "In Truth and Reconciliation, First Things First— The Truth," *Yes!*, August 16, 2017, http://www .yesmagazine.org/peace-justice/in-truth-and -reconciliation-first-things-first-the-truth-20170817.
5   Sarah van Gelder, "The Radical Work of Healing: Fania and Angela Davis on a New Kind of Civil Rights Activism, *"Yes!*, February 18, 2016 http: //www.yesmagazine.org/issues/life-after-oil/the -radical-work-of-healing-fania-and-angela-davis -on-a-new-kind-of-civil-rights-activism-20160218.
6   Randall Robinson, *The Debt: What America Owes to Blacks* (New York: Dutton, 2000), 9.
7   Chicago Torture Justice Center: http://chicago torturejustice.org/.
8   The CTTT Reparations Guide can be downloaded for free at the CTTT website. It is considered a living document, a work in progress. If you have questions or suggestions for additional reparative actions and/or resources, you can contact the Reparations Working Group through the "contact" page on the CTTT website: http://coming

tothetable.org/wp-content/uploads/2018/01
/Reparations_Guide_Jan2018.pdf.
9   White Ally Toolkit: https://www.whiteallytoolkit.com/.
10 Showing Up for Racial Justice: http://www.showing
upforracialjustice.org/.

Chapter 9: Liberation and Transformation
1   *Traces of the Trade: A Story from the Deep North* (Ebb Pod Productions, 2008), http://www.traces ofthetrade.org/.
2   Dalai Lama, Desmond Tutu, and Douglas Abrams, *The Book of Joy: Lasting Happiness in a Changing World* (New York: Avery, 2016), 59–60.

Acknowledgments

The authors wish to express our deep gratitude to our editor, Barb Toews, for her wisdom and support in crafting this Little Book. Thanks to Carl Stauffer and Howard Zehr of the Zehr Institute for Restorative Justice and to our friends at the Center for Justice and Peacebuilding at Eastern Mennonite University for your encouragement; Dionne Ford, Lynda Davis, and Fabrice Guerrier for reviewing and improving the manuscript; and Kay Pranis, Katie Mansfield, Hannah Kelley, Elaine Zook Barge, Johonna Turner, Carolyn Yoder, David Anderson Hooker, damali ayo, Jolandi Steven, Stephanie Carter, Lee Tilson, and many CTTT friends for inspiration and support. We thank Jada Mica Drew for her mentorship and magic; Fania Davis for her care, intention, and service to the work of racial justice; and Cassandra Lane, Danita Rountree Green, David Beumee, Dr. Ruth Baskerville, Lauren Davis, Leslie Stainton, Sarah Jenkins, Sharon Morgan, Sheri Bailey, Sri Lalitambika Devi, and Kimberly James for writing such powerful, illustrative sidebar stories. We're sorry they all wouldn't fit within these pages and look forward to sharing them in other formats so all can benefit from your stories.

About the Authors

Jodie and Tom have worked together since 2016, when they co-facilitated a breakout session at a restorative justice conference. They collaborated with others to develop curriculum for *The Coming to the Table Approach: A Racial Healing & Social Justice Training Workshop*, an ongoing training program they co-facilitate. This book reflects what they've taught and learned over the past three years. One hundred percent of the royalties from this Little Book are donated to Coming to the Table to support ongoing racial healing work. To inquire with questions, or about training workshops, write to Jodie and Tom through www.comingtothetable.org/lbrh.

Group Discounts for

The Little Book of
Racial Healing
ORDER FORM

If you would like to order multiple copies of *The Little Book of Racial Healing* for groups you know or are a part of, please email **bookorders@ skyhorsepublishing.com** or fax order to **(212) 643-6819**. (Discounts apply only for more than one copy.)

Photocopy this page and the next as often as you like.

The following discounts apply:

1 copy	$5.99
2-5 copies	$5.39 each (a 10% discount)
6-10 copies	$5.09 each (a 15% discount)
11-20 copies	$4.79 each (a 20% discount)
21-99 copies	$4.19 each (a 30% discount)
100 or more	$3.59 each (a 40% discount)

Free Shipping for orders of 100 or more!

Prices subject to change.

Quantity   *Price*   *Total*

                         The Little Book of

_____ copies of   *Racial Healing* @   _____   _____

(Standard ground shipping costs will be added for orders of less than 100 copies.)

METHOD OF PAYMENT

❒   Check or Money Order
       (*payable to* **Skyhorse Publishing** *in U.S. funds*)

❒   Please charge my:
❒ MasterCard ❒ Visa
❒ Discover   ❒ American Express
_____

Exp. date and sec. code_____

Signature _____

Name _____

Address _____

City_____

State _____

Zip_____

Phone_____

Email _____

SHIP TO: (if different)
Name _____

Address _____

City_____

State _____

Zip_____

Call: (212) 643-6816
Fax: (212) 643-6819
Email: bookorders@skyhorsepublishing.com
(do not email credit card info)